Advanced Praise for

"Through this book and her own path to personal reinvention, Natalie reminds us that before we move forward, we often have to look back. Let Her Out enables all of us to think deeply about our personal brand, values, and how we want to be known in the world."

— Dorie Clark, author of *Reinventing You* and executive education faculty, Duke University Fuqua School of Business

"Have you ever wondered what happened to that unabashed, unapologetic, unrepentant you from your childhood? Natalie Siston goes on a journey to find her younger, bolder self, and teaches you in the process how she Let Her Out… and how you can, too."

— Laura Gassner Otting - Washington Post Best Selling Author of *Limitless: How to Ignore Everybody, Carve Your Own Path, and Live Your Best Life*

"Let Her Out is a heartfelt and thought-provoking reminder for each of us to dig deep and return to our truest selves. The powerful questions for the reader's own reflection will mine some old memories and new motivation to remember who you have always been."

— Katie Rasoul, Author of *Hidden Brilliance*, Speaker, Coach, Founder - Team Awesome Coaching

"Whether it's a Her or a Him, we all have parts of ourselves dying to come out. Literally dying. Suffocating from years and perhaps decades of expectations and fear covering up our deepest authenticity. In Let Her Out, Natalie not only gives you permission, but encourages you to let out the best version of yourself buried beneath layers of social conditioning. She demonstrates and challenges us to do this in the context of her real and relatable real life. After all, what good do the triumphant stories of a few really do? Sure, they're inspiring and moving, but the reality is, as Natalie points out, the lessons buried in our ordinary lives are actually the most extraordinary. I'm confident you'll find this book relatable on many levels."

— Jeffrey Shaw, Small Business Consultant, host of The Self Employed Life podcast, author of *LINGO*

"As Natalie's third grade teacher (my first year of teaching), I can attest that she was a profound thinker, and indeed "kind and good and smart." Thankfully, we have reconnected during my last year of teaching, and it seems our roles have been reversed. This book hit nerve after nerve as I connected not only to Natalie's advice, but also her life. Her words are insightful, wise and inspiring, and I look forward to reconnecting to my version of "Her" in retirement."

— Kristen Caudill, Second Grade Teacher, Seneca East Elementary

"Can you remember that version of your younger self that had big goals and plans? She was energetic, joyful, and ready to take on life! Natalie Siston's remarkable book, Let Her Out, helps you identify that version of you and then offers strategies to reconnect with that spirit. Through her diaries kept throughout her life, Natalie shares her own journey of rediscovering the person she was meant to be, and in doing so, encourages each of us to Let Her Out! Highly recommended."

— Cathy Fyock, Author, *The Speaker Author*

"Too often we forget who we *really* are. As women, we are socialized to prioritize everyone else's needs above our own. Natalie Siston helps us find who we are again through her own story and thought-provoking coaching questions. If you are wrestling with finding purpose, this is the book for you."

— Julie Kratz, CEO of Next Pivot Point,
Expert on Diversity & Allyship, TEDx Speaker, 3-Time author

"One word: Powerful. The stories, concepts, and exercises in this book can change lives, relationships, and careers. Natalie has created a way to unlock who you can be in the present and future by leveraging who you've always been, making the work completely personal to each reader. This magic makes it accessible to everyone, wherever they are on their journey. Highly recommended."

— Shawn Homan, Financial Services Executive,
magic aficionado, strong ally to those Letting Her Out

"So many of the stories Natalie shared in her book provided me with a warm recollection of many things I did when I was little, and her actionable prompts reminded me to reflect on who I currently am, and to ensure that I am always showing up as my true self. This is an excellent read for women out there who are feeling like they're missing that spark in their lives; through this book, you will be able to re-activate that spark that's hiding within."

— Apryl Z. Schlueter, Get it Done Guru & Chief Energy! Officer, The Cheerful Mind, Inc.

"I'm grateful Natalie's journey to find herself allowed us to reconnect. She took 'brain' knowledge and passionately pursued it with her heart, allowing her to soar! In Let Her Out: Reclaim Who You Have Always Been, she eloquently reaches out to your heart. LISTEN to and LIVE by her words!"

— Bruce Boguski – Author, Motivational Speaker and President of The Winner's Edge

"This is just the book I needed to read right now as I enter midlife and find myself yearning to reconnect to the creativity, boldness, spunk, and thirst for knowledge I had as a young child and teenager. Natalie's story-telling, mixed with her inspiration, encouragement, and outlined steps for how to move forward, have already made an impact on how I'm showing up in the world. I'm grateful she is leading the charge to motivate women everywhere to LET HER OUT!"

— Abbey Jo Griffith, Founder, Uplifted Learning Hometown: Archbold, Ohio (population: 4,300)

"Being a small town girl myself, *Let Her Out* helped me to reconnect to my roots and reminded me that anything is possible. By setting my goals and uncovering my own barriers and truths, I too can make my hopes and dreams become my reality."

— Olivea Heather Renée Oldham, Fortune 100 communications expert, small town girl from Baltimore, Ohio (Population 3,015)

"Natalie uses her rural upbringing to help you address big problems. The reader gets to decide what are the big problems in HER life and use the questions to help in a deep-dive to find solutions. This method will generate feelings from your past to move forward and allow you to grow."

— Jessica Weitthoff, Associate, JP Morgan Chase

Dedication

To Mom and Dad,
For never questioning what I thought was possible

To Rob,
For filling more pages of my diary than you'll ever know

To Mary Beth & Katie,
For giving me a reason to never hold back

To Nicci,
For being by my side as much of this journey unfolded

Contents

Preface

We emerged from the creek (pronounced crick where I come from) covered head-to-toe in mud. Upon entering the house, we were ushered directly into the bathtub, where we continued to have the best day of our lives. We recounted making our "witches brew" filled with the finest mud found in Seneca County, Ohio, newly fallen leaves that signaled the beginning of fall, and an assortment of branches, rocks, and twigs found on the forest floor. My sister, Nicci, neighbor, Gretchen, and I were living our lives big, messy, and unapologetically. We weren't concerned about the checkboxes of life. We weren't stressed about the next thing on the to-do list. We woke up every day and lived as we were always meant to be.

This normal day in the life of Natalie Jean Powell is the type of memory I bring to mind when the days of adulthood seem heavy, burdensome and unfair. I look into Her eyes and remind myself that I am powerful; I am worthy; I am living a meaningful life.

Here is how I remember my eight-year old self:

Knobby knees.
Bowl-cut hair.
Clear voice.
Bright eyes.
Spunky personality.
Unending curiosity.
Limitless imagination.
Unshaken confidence.
Endless compassion.

On the following pages, not only will you dig into the depths of *my* Her, but you will be invited to write the story of *your* Her. She has never left you. The effort you'll take to dig beneath the surface to get to her power, her spirit, and her heart will be worth it when you are able to reclaim who you have always been and live a life full of head-to-toe mud and endless ideas for making today (and tomorrow) the best day it can be.

Why do we need to Let Her Out?

Two shoe boxes traveled with me from college dorm room to college dorm room. They came with me to the tiny apartments in California where I started my post-college and newlywed life and eventually to the home where I started my family. These boxes contained the story of my life as told to "Dear Diary" from the age of eight to 25. Even though these boxes made each move, I never opened them. I was scared. I was scared because if I opened the covers, I would be reminded of HER. You know Her. She is the confident one. The one who had a million dreams. The one who wanted to be President. The one who wouldn't take "no" for an answer.

For 15 years, I let those books remain in those boxes. Then, on the eve of my 40th birthday, I decided it was time to open them. It was time to be reminded of Her, to reconnect to Her, remove the barriers to Her, and, ultimately, to Let Her Out.

For a long time, I didn't think my life was tragic or triumphant enough to be published in a book and shared with the world. I am a normal wife, mom, and business owner. I haven't overcome an addiction, made a million dollars overnight, or walked a red carpet. However, from the moment I read the first line in the Hello Kitty diary I started at age eight, I knew this story had to be told. While 75% of what I read was cringeworthy (oh, all of the crushes on boys I had long forgotten about), the other 25% was pure gold. What I realized while reading the lines I wrote so long ago was that my life has probably been more similar to the majority of women in America - and the world - in its lack of tragedy and triumph than the life of the latest bestselling author or motivational speaker. I think you will resonate with the lessons, laughs and tears I uncovered in those shoe boxes. Here are some of the lines that made me realize this was worth sharing:

> *...It's not how a person looks. It's how they act [that matters].*
> *...If I'm ever poor in money, I'm still rich if I have my best friend.*
> *...Love is sacrificing an intimate relationship in order to allow a friendship to blossom.*
> *...Tranquility is falling in love before the first kiss. Falling is the kiss.*
> *...Faith is forgetting about the past, setting aside the future, and enjoying the present.*

No matter the age of the person who wrote those things, they're magical. When I read the words I wrote so long ago, my heart broke for the young girl who thought she had to hang out with different people, look a different way, or be someone who she wasn't. My heart also swelled because, in between those lines of writing, I saw beauty. I saw intelligence. I saw the person I am today. Reading these words reminded me that we have to be who we've always been in order to become who we never thought we would be.

The same amount of wisdom was in a 15-year old girl growing up in a small rural Ohio town as in the young woman who started her career in Silicon Valley and the person who became a Fortune 100 leader, entrepreneur and mother.

What follows is my story. While this is my story, part of it will also be your story. As it unfolds, I ask you to come along with me and let your inner girl come out. Together, we will:

- Remember Her
- Reconnect to Her
- Remove Barriers to Her
- Let Her Out

The reason I'm publishing this book at the age of 40 is that I wish I hadn't spent so many of my trips around the sun trying to impress people, convince myself that I wasn't good enough, or settle into the background when I knew I was meant to be on stage. I wish I had spent more time *living* the words I wrote in the privacy of my small town bedroom, my first apartment, and the house where I now raise my two little girls. <u>I wish I had spent more time being who I</u> <u>already was, instead of trying to become someone I *thought* I should be.</u>

I wish I had spent more time being who I already
was, instead of trying to become someone I thought
I should be.

Over the past few years, I've gotten to know my inner small town girl more than I ever thought I would. After realizing that everything I learned to be successful in business came from growing up in a town of 600 people, I started a company called Small Town Leadership to share those lessons with organizations and leaders from around the world. I help organizations and leaders develop the type of culture and skills that will allow them to make their company feel like a small town. I describe this culture as a place where everyone knows everyone, everyone's work matters, and there is a sense of care and camaraderie that's necessary to survive *and* thrive. I also show them that small town doesn't mean small minded and invite them to embrace diversity and inclusion. These ingredients are often what is missing when a company isn't performing well or when people don't feel connected to their work.

What it took to get this book in your hands (or on your tablet or audiofeed) was a coach asking me the same questions I will pose to you throughout the following pages. She asked me, "What do you miss doing from when you were a child?" "What lit you up?" The answer I gave to her floated off my tongue without hesitation. I told her what I missed most, and when I felt the most alive, was when I was speaking and writing.

Since that coaching session, over five years ago, I began speaking and writing more than I had in a long time. Uncovering my diaries and essays felt like winning the lottery because they are informing my work in ways I couldn't anticipate. Reading the words from my younger self reminded me that I have *always been* who I was meant to be. You have always been who you were meant to be, too.

You have always been who you were meant
to be, too.

Somehow, life has gotten in your way. You often wonder: "Where has my inner child gone?" "When does she show up?" "When am I hiding from Her?" "What can I do to bring Her back?"

Throughout this book, I will pose questions and challenges like these to help you become who you are meant to be. What have you always enjoyed doing, especially as a little girl, that you've abandoned in your adolescence and young adulthood? Were you always the first one to get onto the basketball court during a pick-up game? Then, go lace up your shoes and get back in the game. Did you play the starring role in the school musical and the only place you sing now is in the shower? What would it be like to get back on stage on your campus or in your community? Were you always carrying a notebook around to capture your deepest thoughts or observations about the interactions happening around you? What have you written lately to express yourself? Even if you were too scared to step on stage in your youth, or life handed you challenges that made you grow up too fast to experience the things I will reveal in this book, she is in there waiting to be let out.

hoarder

Here is my rallying cry as you work through the stories, reflections, exercises and questions that follow: Let HER out *every day*. Do not hold back. When you share your gifts, even the ones that haven't seen the light of day since you were a child, you will feel more whole. When you say the words that are deep in your heart out loud to those around you, you and everyone you encounter on your trips around the sun will be better.

When you share your gifts, even the ones that
haven't seen the light of day since you were a child,
you will feel more whole.

Be who you have always been, and do not hold back. I want to live in a world where SHE is out. A world where your dreams don't die because the next report or the next baby is due. A world where your dreams are big, your plans are bigger, and your actions are massive. A world where your voice is clear, compelling, and filled with conviction.

I am honored to be on this journey with you to Let Her Out.

How to Use This Book

From the outside, this probably looks like a book that you can easily get through in a solid afternoon of reading, a cross-country flight, or a week of bedtime reading sessions. While I might be breaking every rule of authorhood by encouraging you NOT to binge this book, that's what I'm going to do. This is a *150*-page life story intertwined with life coaching. Interspersed throughout are over 100 coaching questions that allow you to Pause, Reflect, and in some cases, Take Action. I want you to approach this book with these things in mind.

This book is broken down into four sections, with an intermission at the halfway point. Throughout each of these sections, the coaching questions will invite you to dig into your past as well as envision your future. This book is best read section by section, allowing yourself time at the end of each section to work through the questions. Here are some suggestions to make the most of your experience reading the book.

1. **Use the guide.** Download the free Let Her Out book guide at www. letherout.com/resources. The guide outlines all of the questions and exercises provided in the book. If you are borrowing the book from the library or want to keep your personal copy pristine and free of notes, this is for you!

2. **Find a reading partner.** You will get the most out of this book by sharing the experience with someone else. Ask a friend, your sister, or even your mom, to jump into this journey with you. Work section by section and share with one another. Consider asking someone who knew you "way back when" to join you on the journey.

3. **Book club, anyone?** If your book club enjoys diving into personal development, this would be a great pick. I also share enough stories from the way-back machine for your group to get to know one another in a

new and different way. There's even a special book club guide at www.
letherout.com/resources.

4.   **Employee Resource Group Read.** Does your company sponsor a
     women's resource group? I can't think of a better place for this to come
     to life, and for you to subsequently challenge all of the women around
     you to Let Her Out, than at work.

5.   **Engage on Social Media.** Connect with me on any of the channels
     and be sure to tag me or add the hashtag #letheroutbook to share your
     experiences.

For all of the men reading this book: You can simply replace "Her" with
"Him" and dive in. If you are reading this in support of your spouse, partner,
sister or colleague, use this book as an opportunity to engage in dialogue about
Her experience and how she can bring more of Her to every situation and cir-
cumstance. While this is my experience, there are elements that every woman
will relate to as she attempts to reconnect with and revive Her.

Special Note: If you have experienced significant trauma in your life, make
sure you are walking through this book with the appropriate care. I have not
experienced, nor will reflect on, any significant personal trauma, but for you,
certain stories and exercises could stir up memories from the past that are best
suited to discuss with a therapist or trained mental health professional.

Above all, enjoy yourself. I've had more fun remembering Her than I have
in a long time. I hope you have a similar experience. Share it with someone you
care about. Share your experience, using the hashtag #letheroutbook on any of
the socials.

Section 1

REMEMBER HER

Remember Her

The first step to take on our journey to let her out is to Remember Her. This process has been easy for me because of that stack of diaries I've been holding onto, not to mention the scrapbooks I made for grades 1-12, the cabinet full of photo albums my parents have kept since before I was born, and the general memorabilia that slowly made its way to my house, one box at a time, while my parents converted my childhood bedroom into a crafting space. It doesn't matter whether you have access to ten boxes of archives or simply the seared-in-your-brain memories that come from childhood: Use what you have to remember Her. There are four ways I'm going to invite you to reconnect. I'll bring you into my story in order to see how this unfolds. These are through photos, diary entries, reliving experiences from your youth and tapping into memories and emotions that can only be felt by Her.

CHAPTER 1

Remembering through Photos

The first way to remember is through photos. One of the first things I did after launching Small Town Leadership was to spend an afternoon at my parents' house, going through photo albums and digitizing shots that could be used on the website. I was looking for pictures that represented small town living, to include in the background of the site. Instead, what I found were pictures of the Her that I had forgotten. There were silly pictures of me when I was a small child, with my mom's pantyhose pulled up to my chest, photos of me rocking out with the drum set my grandparents proudly presented to me for my sixth birthday, and more pictures than I could recall of my sister, Nicci, and me in all forms of dress-up, make-up, hair curlers and perms. The reason I had forgotten about these moments was because my life got filled up with box checking and going after the next thing I thought was expected of me.

Looking at these photos, I began to remember Her. A few key moments stick out from this photo journey, when I was playing full out as a girl and young woman. Here are a few snapshots in time that allow me to remember Her when I feel like the world is suffocating and unforgiving.

Zestfully Clean – When I was ten, I went to summer camp with other girls whose parents worked at National Machinery, a major employer at the time in Tiffin, Ohio. On skit night, our cabin decided to act out popular commercials on TV that summer. Without hesitation, I volunteered to be the "Zestfully Clean" girl (If you don't know what I'm talking about, hit up Google). This involved wearing my bathing suit in front of the whole camp and pretending to sing in the shower. For a woman who now hesitates to bare her midriff at the local pool, this was a refreshing reminder that I am still the same girl who eagerly volunteered to put herself confidently on display in front of a group of my peers.

Chuckwagon sidekick – Around the same time, my family took a trip to the Grand Canyon. One evening, we attended a chuckwagon dinner, complete with square dancing and bonfire. I came dressed for the occasion in blue jeans and a cowgirl hat. Upon seeing my full themed attire, one of the "real cowboys" invited me to sit on the front of the wagon with him, and later I was his dancing partner. I tried to follow along as he showed me how to do certain steps in front of the entire crowd. I don't remember if I followed the moves correctly, but I do remember the feeling of throwing caution to the wind in front of an audience of other vacationing strangers.

County Fair royalty – The summer before I went to college, I competed for the title of Seneca County Fair queen. I didn't win, but was part of the queen's court. This granted me and the other members of the court free run of the fairgrounds. We handed out trophies and ribbons, announced 4-H competitors, and performed other assorted duties that required someone wearing a sash. The final day of the fair, in a combination of exhaustion and adrenaline, I participated in a sandwich-eating contest, followed by a square dancing demonstration. I remember getting flung all over the dusty barn by other members of the fair court, not caring about a thing in the world. My stomach was full and my pride was restored from not winning the queen's title. I spent most of the week leading up to this moment feeling stung by not winning the crown and hesitating before putting on the runner-up sash; the moments of bonding, over cold-cut sandwiches and square dances that none of us knew, reminded me of what was important about that summer.

Bringing back these memories reminds me of the Her who was living without a concern about how I looked, who saw me acting silly or if I messed up the dance moves. Unfortunately, she was the one who retreated with each passing year because of concern over failing, constant striving for perfection, and being caught in the whirlwind of so much on the to-do list.

Remembering Her through photos leads me to ask: What if each of us showed up like this every day? Imagine if we danced without knowing the moves, if we held our shoulders high, no matter who was watching, and we kept a smile on our face the whole time?

Pause, Reflect & Take Action: Photos of Her

- Action Item: Where can you find pictures of Her? If you don't have access to photos, what images can help you remember Her?

- Once you locate pictures, find one that truly represents Her as you wish to remember Her. What about Her in this picture do you appreciate?

- What about Her do you see in yourself today?

Once you've found a picture or identified an image that helps you remember Her the most, print it or put a digital copy on your phone. In moments when the world feels like it's closing in on you, look at Her. She is there to remind you that she never went anywhere.

Chapter 2

Remembering through Diary Entries

The most powerful way I've been able to remember Her is by reading my diaries: It's what inspired this book in the first place. When I got beyond the gut-wrenching parts, I was able to remember Her in a way I would never have anticipated. Here are some moments from four different periods of my life that stand frozen in time. Some are my proudest moments. Some are my saddest moments. No matter the mood, they paint the picture that who she was then is who I am today. I had no idea when I wrote these words that they would become the key to remembering Her and ultimately, letting Her out.

In elementary school, the Her I remember most is the girl who was compassionate, caring, and solid in her beliefs. On November 25, 1990 (age 10) I wrote out all of the lyrics to *Proud to Be an American* and prayed that the *"people would get out of Saudia Arabia any day."* Around that same time, I was faced with the death of a close family friend and simply said, *"I don't think she will make it out of the hospital alive."* The heaviness of those thoughts and words reminds me of a child who felt with her whole heart and loved unconditionally. She was confident in herself, yet unsure about the wider world.

During junior high, notes of achievement and disappointment intertwined. I ran for class president, but was defeated by my best friend. I won all of the awards there were to win when it came to music and academics. Some days, I would feel like the world was out to get me, but most days, I was floating in my own orbit. Of my confirmation during eighth grade, I said, *"I never realized just how much the people in the church care for me. I have received so many cards and gifts from church members that I was overwhelmed! I'm upset that it took me so long to realize that. I think I'm becoming more of a dreamer. I can see myself in a better light! It feels good to truly know yourself and like yourself."* To know yourself AND like yourself. Those are tall orders coming from my 14-year-old self.

High school is when I remember the Her that makes my heart beat proudly in my body. My sister and I were always close, and it was at the age of 14 that I said, *"Today I realized how proud of my sister I am. She got up in front of the church and explained about General Synod (the largest gathering of the United Church of Christ in the country). I want to make the people in Republic proud of my sister and me. Deep down I have the ambition and spunk it takes to be something big. I want to share all of this desperately with someone."*

The word 'Ambition' will hold a special meaning throughout this book. It's the word that shepherded me from age 39 into 40; the word that so many women are told to let go of, or certainly not have too much of, has been inside me this whole time. The other word that made me laugh out loud was 'spunk'. In a recent interaction with a master coach, he said he liked my spunk. It's no coincidence that, when we start to let our inner 14-year-old out, others can see Her so clearly.

Ambition and dreaming big continued to be a theme early in high school. During a church conference I attended when I was 15, I wrote several letters to God. In one of them, I said, *"I want so much out of life. Not only do I want so much to succeed in the eyes of my fellow man, but I want the world to know that Natalie Jean Powell isn't just a small town girl. She has a heart, a brilliant mind, and a giving spirit. I know my future will come together, but it won't be without the help of you."* I'm not sure if I ever spoke these words out loud to my friends or family. I'm sure people sensed this burgeoning desire to make it big, but for most of my life, the thoughts have been relegated to these private diary entries. In turn, those desires to play big were snuffed out, and I kept safe and small.

It was around the same time of my life when I wrote the following, *"I've been battling this past year with a lot more than I let be known. I felt fat. I hated my zits. Now I don't feel fat and my zits are going away."* These two sentences held more power in my life at that time than I remembered. I'm sure they are things most teenage girls think and feel. What makes me proud of the Her that had the guts to write these two sentences is that I worked hard to make the changes I sought in my life. I began exercising regularly. I asked my mom if I could go to the doctor and get help with my acne. This was an emerging woman who sought change, acted on it, and made it happen. It wasn't about vanity. It was about confidence and taking control of myself.

High school continued to be about identity building and allowing myself to feel all of the feelings that come along with it. My sophomore year was especially meaningful, as it was the year when I had my first long-term boyfriend. He was someone I could both laugh with and share a serious moment. There were so many facets of that relationship that I was reminded of by reading diary pages from that time. He introduced me to Garth Brooks and took me to my first concert. (To this day, the 1996 Garth Brooks Fresh Horses tour is hard to top.) Even though we were a year apart in school, we were in the same drivers education class and compared notes as we prepared to take our written and on-road exams. More than anything, he showed me that when you care about someone deeply enough, you will always find room for them in your life.

At the same time I was learning about romantic relationships, our high school was shocked by the death of one of our classmates in a tragic car accident. When your high school is made up of only 350 people, this type of experience hits everyone to the core. I reflected a few weeks after this happened by saying, *"I have felt so much in the past day, week, month and year. I've felt more love, more sadness, more hope, more compassion than I feel I can take. My life is so full I feel like I'm brimming with the hope and the love that I feel. I want to share that so bad. I just don't know how. My words speak, my actions are louder, but if I could just get people inside my mind, they would feel what I feel."*

At the beginning of my junior year in high school, a motivational speaker came for a kick-off assembly. He told us how to capture our dreams and believe in ourselves. At that moment, I knew something special was happening in my life. *"I learned that I'm in the 3% bracket of Americans today. Americans who write down their goals. That is part of my life and I know it will lead to success. Success wherever I may find it - in money, business, music, love. I'll appreciate it in whatever form I get it."*

Remembering this moment led me to the many loose-leaf pages that were tucked alongside the diaries in those shoe boxes. On these pages were lists of goals from 1996, 1997, and 1998. They ranged from "get the lead in the school musical" to "earn a superior at the science fair competition."

On a whim, I reached out to the speaker, Bruce Boguski, who is now 74-years-old and is still motivating audiences. What I didn't realize when I watched him on stage over 24 years ago is that he was in the profession that I wanted so badly to understand. For all of this time, Bruce has been an abstract example of who I wanted to be like when I grew up. Not only did I connect to his message, but somewhere deep inside me, I knew I would one day be on similar stages, helping other people lean into their dreams. Speaking with him in the twilight of his career confirmed for me that, when we follow our passion, we can weather any storm. Now that our paths have intersected again, we are helping each other craft goals and plans to reach them. We are never done learning and growing.

Even though I was gaining confidence in my ability to set and achieve goals, I had a hard time releasing control of situations. As our high school prepared to put on our production of *Grease* during my junior year, I was trying hard to prepare myself for rejection. *"I have a major thought on my mind: Life is not all about first prize. It isn't all about being the leading role. There can be only one winner and only one leading part. I think our world would be a much better place if everyone could understand that. So when they post the musical list tomorrow, I will remember that there can only be one Rizzo, one Danny, and one Sandy. Because sometimes the world is unfair. That is life and you get hit with it everyday."*

What happened the following day is that I didn't come in first, nor did I even get a named part. I was just a Pink Lady. *"I don't even know how to describe my emotions. At first, I was angry, then I got upset, then I was mad. Now I'm just accepting. I don't know where I get that calming effect. I have no idea. Maybe there is a little angel looking over me, keeping me calm, safe and peaceful. I've learned that life is tough, but there are streaks of happiness that make it all worthwhile. So I will make my part in the musical stick out. I'm not playing in the background this year. I will do something to be remembered. I guess there are stages of acceptance in life. I've been blessed with grace in acceptance."*

The phrase that sticks out to me most in this passage is "streaks of happiness." How many of us are actively looking for and appreciating streaks of happiness in our day-to-day lives? My reward for this newfound acceptance and enjoyment of streaks of happiness was to be given a second chance. Over Christmas break, the girl who was supposed to play Jan moved away and the part was up for grabs. I never considered myself as the comic, goofy lead, but when it came time to prove my worth for the role, I showed up to win. To this day, playing Jan has been my favorite role. I made spaghetti twirling an active part of the opening scene, developed a serious Twinkie addiction, and learned how wonderful it felt to make people laugh.

How many of us are actively looking for and appreciating streaks of happiness in our day-to-day lives?

For all of the laughs I generated on that stage, I also had a remarkable level of seriousness at the age of 17. During a conversation with my best friend, I said the following and recounted it in my diary. *"I am so deep. I am sitting at the bottom of the ocean staring at the beautiful fish and searching for a certain treasure. While I am busy searching, others are still standing on the dock with the sun in their eyes. They are blind and afraid to jump in. I will forever bask in the deepness of treasure and thoughts, while others just stand and wait for the sun to go down."* It was always clear to me that I had many layers. I wasn't drawn to petty gossip or passing fads. I was the girl to come to when you had a major life issue to discuss. I understood this and wanted to lean into the care, concern and compassion I had for my friends and classmates. Going into my senior year, I said, *"In my senior year, I want to be the shoulder they lean on. For I know where I am going - and I want to lead the way for those who can't find their path. Some won't want to be shown the way, but will be thankful when they get through safely."*

When I read these words today, what screams out at me is: the life coach emerges. I have always been the steady and level-headed one. I have always had an intuitive connection to other people, to sense what motivates them, and to show them what's possible. The irony in this emerging strength of propping others up is that it intersected with a time of my life when I started to have doubts about who I was becoming.

I wrote two of the most profound diary entries as I prepared to leave Republic, Ohio for The Ohio State University.

August 28, 1998 (age 18) - I think a lot about the passage of time. Minutes into hours. Hours into days. Days into weeks. Weeks into months. Months into a year. Years into forever. It is an obsession. What I do to consume time determines who I will be in the years that will form my life. It's now the point in my life when I decide what to do with the majority of my time. Study, party, communicate, play music, meditate, exercise. God creates people and makes circumstances happen in their lives, but once this initial event occurs, it is then up to the individuals to control their lives. That's what I'm trying to do. I'm trying to control my own life while still having an impact on others' lives. I don't know how I will impact lives starting in two weeks. For the past 13 years I've been a student, a teacher, a scholar and a mentor. I never want to stop learning and I still want to be a teacher. When Tracy, my piano student of two years, told me she wants to be a singer and when she dedicated her piano solo to me, I glowed. She started out as a shy, timid girl from a modest family. Because I've stepped into her life and made her feel like an important person, she now has dreams and aspirations. So I will never stop being a teacher. As far as being a pupil, I will listen to great scholars, yet I will question their deep think- ing. I have the gift of innovative thinking and reasoning. I will always treasure and share this gift. So the passage of time means me developing into a stellar scholar and teacher. It also means a time for new characters in the timeless book of my own life. The hours, days, weeks, months and years of my life have meshed into one masterpiece. I mean to include every one of the characters in this picture in the rest of my life. Wherever they may be. Whatever part they play in my destiny. Time will tell all!

September 12, 1998 (age 18) - What will tomorrow bring? After 18 years of living in a protected world, in a controlled and chaperoned envi- ronment, I am free. I'm scared, for I have no clue what tomorrow, this week, or this year have in store. I know that my band audition will determine my fall quarter. I know that the friends I make the first week on campus might dictate how my life turns out. Ohio State has always been this dis- tant, blurred dream. It has been put into focus occasionally by tours, visits and orientation, but now it is time for the real deal. In my heart I take with me so much. In my mind I have knowledge that will be expanded and tested more now than it ever has been. In my soul I take me. My optimism. My faith. My hope. My love. Each piece of me that I take to OSU will become blended into the campus quilt. I pray that it is a beautiful quilt.

With interesting designs and a myriad of colors. This masterpiece must be diverse and spectacular. It is a quilt that I want to take a piece of when I leave OSU. A piece of the quilt. To cover up with in the cool night air. To share with the one I love. The quilt will color my world. Now it's time to begin putting my pieces in!

The words that stick out to me in these passages are impact, innovative thinking, and masterpiece. I was called at the age of 18 to make a difference, be creative, and create something with the gifts I had been given, but because this thing I wanted to do wasn't on a list of college majors, I couldn't articulate what it was.

October 7, 1998 (Age 18) - Every day I wonder what I want to do for the rest of my life. All I really want to do is to touch other's lives. Make them see the clear path ahead of them. Open doors they've never noticed before. I don't know what kind of major offers that outlet. I just want to learn everything I can. I want to absorb knowledge. I want to succeed, but most importantly, learn. College is more of a personal growth experience than a learning experience, or so said a senior. I think that is so true. I'm ready for new branches and deeper roots.

June 17, 1999 (age 19): Sometimes I feel like that is my calling in life. Teach people how to do what they think they cannot do. Help them think outside the box. Spark a flame inside.

It's amazing that I didn't come to the conclusion of what I wanted to be when I grew up after an undergraduate degree, MBA, and thirteen jobs at six companies. I had to read what I wrote when I was eighteen years old to remember that the speaker, writer and coach has been in there the whole time. I have been leaving a trail of breadcrumbs behind me my whole life that only in retrospect come together to form the identity I recognize when I look into the mirror. For too long, instead of reminding myself of these breadcrumbs, anecdotes, and clues, I told myself that "I am not" these things. I am not a motivational speaker. I am not a women's empowerment leader. I am not an inspirational writer. Instead, I told myself I needed to be who corporate America or the general population wanted me to be. Now I know I can throw all of that out the window and rewind to where the bread loaf was whole and reclaim being a motivator, women's leader and inspiration to whoever crosses my path.

I have been leaving a trail of breadcrumbs behind me my whole life that only in retrospect come together to form the identity I recognize when I look into the mirror.

If your remembering allows you to dig into the words you wrote in your youth, look closely for the breadcrumbs you've been leaving behind you your whole life. Even if you don't have these physical reference points, remember the essence of who you have always been. She's still in there. She's simply been told she needs to be someone else. It's up to you to remember Her so you can take back who you want to be.

Pause, Reflect & Take Action: Diaries & Archives

- What diaries, essays, early writings or yearbooks do you have access to in order to remember Her?

- What "All About Me" works can remind you of what she liked, who her friends were, and what she did in her spare time?

- If you didn't keep a journal or don't have access to archives like these, what books or movies from the formative years in your life help you remember Her?

CHAPTER 3

Remembering through Emotional Memories

The next way to remember is through seared-in memories and experiences that made you feel alive and fully yourself. These feelings could range from excitement to anticipation to anger to pride and were the result of specific events or experiences in your young life. When I step back into the following moments, I can feel Her to my core.

Remembering the Song in my Heart

For as long as I can remember, music has been part of my life. Remembering Her would not be complete without the memories of piano lessons, trombone practice or choir rehearsal. I started playing piano in first grade, trombone in fifth, and have been singing as long as I've had vocal chords. I am not a natural born musician, but I love to watch and listen to those born with this gift. Music in my life was practiced and rehearsed and is the basis for the strong discipline I developed as a child. Music was there to comfort me on a hard day or to be played joyfully on happy occasions. Music is also where I started my career as a teacher and leader. It's where I learned important lessons about recognizing my limitations and embracing my gifts.

My sophomore year in high school I was hired as the choir director and accompanist at the Bloomville United Methodist Church. It was a struggle. I wasn't comfortable "going with the flow" of the music while simultaneously directing a group of singers. It was also a lot to handle on top of school, extra curriculars, piano lessons, and having a boyfriend. I'm not one to quit, so I stuck to it. Until the day I was fired. I like to think that the main reason for the firing was that the minister's daughter moved back to town and was called in to take over, but part of me also believes it was because I wasn't good at the job. Whatever the reasons, I was fired for the first time when I was 15 years old.

I learned as much from that experience as possible. Soon after getting fired, I quit taking piano lessons, realizing that I had reached the level I wanted to reach. Instead, I focused on learning how to accompany singers. I learned how to improvise. Instead of practicing classical solo music, I began to play choral and pop music and sang along. In the brief moments of time I had by myself at home, I was usually putting on a concert for our two family dogs. By my senior year in high school, I rotated between singing in and accompanying the school choir. At the same time, the same minister who fired me two years prior called to ask me if I wanted to come back and lead the choir. I said, "Yes!" without hesitation. I was confident. I knew I could figure out whatever music we picked. I was a strong leader and I'd taken the previous two years to sharpen my accompanying skills. I'd like to think I was the best 18-year old church choir director they ever had.

Around the same time I started directing and accompanying the choir, I began offering piano lessons. My students varied. There was the lady from church who added piano playing to her bucket list and I sat with her one night a week for a couple of years. My favorite student was Tracy. She was learning the piano at a good pace, but what I discovered was that she had a beautiful voice. We worked in secret for two months so she could surprise her mom with a solo of "Wind Beneath My Wings" at church. Her mom thought Tracy was going to play a song for the congregation, but instead ended up listening to a song sung especially for her. It was one of the most magical musical moments I've witnessed. Helping Tracy uncover a hidden talent and putting it on full display in front of the congregation allowed everyone in the audience to question what was possible. They had likely made assumptions about what a shy, small town girl who sat in the front pew every Sunday was capable of. On that day, she not only started a new page in her own story, but also shattered their preexisting beliefs about her. That moment confirmed that, no matter the path I chose in life, teaching would be part of it.

Throughout elementary, middle and high school, I played the trombone. The main goal I had was to one day be in The Best Damn Band in The Land

(TBDITL) at The Ohio State University. It's the main reason I selected the trombone in 5th grade and what had me diligently learn the instrument. My trombone playing experience was one where the journey ended up being more important than the destination, as the end of the story is that I didn't make the band at Ohio State, although I did try out.

Playing the trombone took me to band competitions, youth band experiences, the Liberty Bowl, and my favorite part of remembering - The All Ohio State Fair Band. It was another one of those goals I set as a child after seeing the band play on one of my many trips to the fair for 4-H. I said, "I'm going to be in that band someday." Sophomore year, I submitted an application and was accepted, which meant I spent one month of my summer practicing and playing across the Ohio State Fairgrounds. The music was exciting, but the friends were even more memorable.

The crowning jewel of my musical career happened as I closed out high school. After being in *Oklahoma* freshman year as a chorus person, *Sound of Music* sophomore year as Sister Sophia, one of the nuns who sings "How Do You Solve a Problem Like Maria?", and *Grease* junior year as Jan, the comical Pink Lady lead, I was chosen to play Hodel in *Fiddler on the Roof* during my senior year. She is the middle daughter, who falls in love with a rebel and moves to Siberia after he is arrested. This was the first time I had a solo – a song called *Far From The Home I Love*. I sang the solo during a scene between Hodel, her love interest Perchik and her father Tevye.

Our early rehearsals were spent blocking scenes. For those non-theater people, that means you figure out how you will move throughout the scene. I was very excited to block the scene that included my solo. With my sister at college and both parents working, I was at home by myself before and after school. During that time, I would play myself the starting note on the piano and stand in the middle of the living room and pretend that I was on stage performing. On the night that we blocked the scene, we got to the portion where the song was and the musical director, Ron, said, "We can skip the song." My reply was, "Well, actually I've been practicing the song. I can sing it a cappella – is that all right?" He said, "Sure."

I proceeded to sing the solo for the first time in the empty auditorium. I sang with every ounce of emotion and passion I had. At the end of the song, my 2 fellow cast members and the musical director stood in silence. And we all stared at each other. It was then that Ron told me one of the most important lessons I learned in theater. He said, "Natalie, I know you are used to applause, but no one is going to clap at the end of the scene. And if you perform it right, there will probably be silence." He said some scenes are meant to leave the audience silent and breathless and this was one of those scenes. At that moment, that didn't make any sense. After all, this was my senior year, my swan song – my time for a round of applause.

Dress rehearsals came to a close and we prepared for opening night. When my scene came, I once again sang my heart out. And there was silence. Not even my parents clapped. The same situation played out for the remainder of our performances. I'm grateful Ron gave me the advice he did. Because I knew to anticipate the silence, I wasn't disappointed.

What didn't make sense my senior year of high school, now makes perfect sense as a 40-year old woman. There are days when we give it our best; we cook the finest dinner, wrap up the hardest project at work, close the biggest sale of our career, and we want a standing ovation. We want acknowledgement for our hard work. We want a pat on the back. Often, however, we are met with silence. We have to remind ourselves that the only applause we need in our lives comes from within. The rest is icing on the cake we have baked for ourselves.

We have to remind ourselves that the only applause we need in our lives comes from within. The rest is icing on the cake we have baked for ourselves.

Music opened up possibilities I didn't know existed beyond my small town. Not only did finding the song in my heart allow me to travel and meet people I never would have crossed paths with otherwise, but it taught me how to blend passion and discipline together. I knew I would never make it to the stage at Carnegie Hall, but discipline and improvisation have helped me to get onto other stages for different types of performance. As long as, every time I get on stage, I remember the Her who played and sang with every ounce of passion, whoever is sitting in the audience will feel the song in my heart.

> ## Pause, Reflect & Take Action: Remembering the Song in Your Heart
>
> - What was the equivalent of piano lessons, marching band or high school musical for you? What activities brought out the song in your heart?
>
> - What type of music, band, or song allows you to remember Her? Go turn it on!

Remembering Ambition

For the past few years, I've chosen a word to help ground me in my purpose and keep me on track toward my goals. As I mentioned earlier in this section, ambition was my word of the year in 2019. When the following quote by Ralph Waldo Emerson showed up on the calendar on my birthday in mid-January, I knew I chose the right word. *"Without ambition one starts nothing. Without work one finishes nothing. The prize will not be sent to you. You have to win it."* I decided 2019 was the year that I would remember the Her that was ambitious and proud of it. Remembering ambition brings me back to the list of odd jobs I had growing up in Republic, Ohio.

Cleaning crew (1991-1998; ages 11-18) – I cleaned houses and offices growing up. I started out by cleaning my Uncle Bob's basement office for $5. I moved into the commercial cleaning space when my mom's church association office was in need of a scrub down. These jobs were not glamorous, but they could be done on my own schedule and I could crank up the music to whatever level I chose during the shift.

Piano teacher (1994-1998; ages 14-18) – I kept a small rolodex of piano students from 8th-12th grades. I told you about Tracy in the previous section.

Babysitter (summer of 1996; age 16) - I babysat the summer between my sophomore and junior year of college. Note the single season duration of this job.

Church choir director (1995; 1997-1998; age 15; 17-18) – The first (and only) job I've ever been fired from and the only one I've gone back to after departure.

Newspaper Reporter (1997-1998; ages 17-18) - I attended and reported on town council meetings for the small towns surrounding Republic, Ohio.

College custodial crew and Banking specialist (1998; age 18) - The jobs that really speak to ambition were the ones from the summer of 1998. I needed a job between my senior year in high school and college. In Republic, Ohio the options were limited. Kids looking for jobs could work on their family farm (my family sold our farm, so this was out for me), babysit (note my tenure above. I was not eager to sign up again.), work at the local factory (my sister took the factory job, and only one child per family was allowed), work in the fast food industry (I wasn't up for the night and weekend work, given other obligations that summer), so I did what was natural for any kid who had just graduated from high school: I signed up to work the summer custodial crew at a local college, mainly responsible for cleaning the recently vacated dorm rooms.

The work, I could handle. Getting to work at 6:00 a.m. – no problem. Cleaning the most awful crud you can imagine – including scraping boogers off dorm room walls – done. (Yes, just visualize that for a moment.) What I soon learned I could not handle was the work ethic and attitudes of my co-workers. I wanted to be busy all day, but they were content to stretch 15-minute breaks into 30. There was constant complaining. They were not happy with their jobs. I knew this was going to be the longest summer of my life.

One week into the custodial job, I attended a graduation party for one of my classmates. At the party, she was talking about her summer job. I can't remember what job she ended up taking, but what I clearly remember her saying is that she "had to turn down the job at the bank" to do this job. Before I knew what I was doing, I said, "Really, you had to give up a job at the bank? Do you know if they are still looking for someone?" She said she was pretty sure they still needed someone, so I asked her if I could get the phone number for the manager.

That Monday, during my morning break I found a pay phone and called the bank manager. I told him I would be happy to be considered for the job that my classmate had to turn down. Two days later, I clocked out of my custodial shift wearing a skirt and blouse, prepared to interview for the bank job, which

I was offered and began the next week. I remember my custodial co-workers feeling very happy for me. They took me to lunch and wished me well. I simply wished for them to find happiness in their work.

Even though I was only eighteen, this provided me with two of my most significant professional lessons. First, striving to be happy at work is something we should all do, and we each play a part in making this happen. After one week with a disengaged team, I knew I had to remove myself from the situation. This helped in future situations, when I couldn't simply walk away from a job, to help uncover ways to appreciate my work and life.

Second, I learned if I wanted something, to go after it. I tell this story when I lead networking seminars because this is how you create opportunity. For a long time (actually up until writing this book), I referred to this as a lucky break. Right place, right time, with the right action taken. Now, I recognize this as my ambition kicking into gear. I had more to give that summer than scraping boogers off of walls. Deep down, I knew that I was supposed to have that conversation with my classmate. I certainly didn't go to the graduation party thinking it would lead to a different job, but if I hadn't asked questions and been bold about my actions, I would be telling a different story today.

The lesson in all of these jobs is that I went after each of these opportunities. None of them fell in my lap. In one case, I got fired and was humble enough to come back two years later when they called me and my skills had improved.

Remembering this ambition has fueled me during the past four years. During that time, I built my business, worked a full time director-level job at a Fortune 100 financial services company, as well as the more important, but often unspoken jobs of being a wife, mom, daughter, sister and contributor to the community. Before reading that Ralph Waldo Emerson quote, *"Without ambition one starts nothing"*, there were many days when I felt guilt and anxiety over the force that ambition was exerting on my life. After reading that Ralph Waldo Emerson quote, I recognized that letting Her out means unleashing ambition, without hesitation or apology.

Remembering Simplicity

I'm going to take you back to Republic, Ohio to remember Her and my no-frills upbringing. Nothing seems more basic and mundane than grocery shopping, except when you grow up in a town of 600 people. The market in Republic closed when I was in elementary school, which meant the nearest grocery store was 10 miles away. My mom planned carefully and had our grocery shopping routine down to a science. She planned carefully enough so that we only needed to go "Krogering" every two weeks. In the week between, she would make sure we had necessities from the gas station convenience store or make a quick trip to the grocery store when she was in town for work.

I looked forward to our big nights out on the town. Our routine was simple. Every other Friday, we would head to town, the town being Tiffin, Ohio (population 15,000). We had dinner out, either at Wendy's or Pizza Hut if it was "Book It" season; in exchange for reading four books, Pizza Hut provided elementary students with a free personal pan pizza. Then, we would go to Kroger and do our shopping. My sister and I would either tag along as my parents shopped, hoping for something exotic like a can of Pringles or package of Keebler cookies to make it into the cart, or spend time in the magazine aisle, reading *Teen Beat*. Nothing was on demand in this small town and I have the memories to remind me of that.

Contrast this to my current suburban life, where I'm 5 minutes away from two large grocery stores, multiple convenience stores, and restaurants of every style and cuisine. If I forget something or run out mid-week, it's easy to stop at the store and replenish. In addition to the multiple stores within a quick drive, for a few extra dollars, I have the option to do curbside pick-up at my local grocery store. If I don't want to leave my house, I can have Amazon Prime deliver to me in 2 days, or Amazon Now get it to me in an hour. Don't get me wrong: I'm happy that I can take advantage of these technological and operational advances, but it makes me ask myself: has my life gotten so busy that I can't spend an hour a week at the grocery store? If I try curb-side pick-up, will I fill the hour I'm not shopping with more important and memorable activities? Will my kids have the same shopping memories as I have? Or will the world evolve so that they won't stand in the magazine aisle reading about the latest heartthrob while I pick out the week's produce?

These all seem like trivial questions to ask about such a mundane and necessary task. At the root of it, I'm trying hard not to over-complicate my life. The simple, routine parts of life are what I remember from my childhood and connect me to a different part of Her. We don't have to buy extravagant things or have a calendar so full that someone needs to do our shopping for us. In many ways, inserting intentional planfulness allows for more time and space to connect than if everything was outsourced. It's my job to balance living in an on-demand world with small town simplicity.

It's my job to balance living in an on-demand world with small town simplicity.

CHAPTER 4

Remembering by Reliving

Another way we can remember Her is by reliving experiences of our youth through the eyes of our younger siblings, children, family members or friends. You can use their life experiences to remind you of your first day of school, first dance, or when you packed your bags and left for college.

Four years ago, I sent my daughter off on the big yellow school bus for the first time. In that moment, while I choked back tears, I was reminded of my first days of school. Next to Christmas, the first day of school was my second favorite day of the year. I loved shopping for new school supplies and a back-pack. I carefully planned my outfit. I had a hard time sleeping before the first day of school.

Even at a young age, I loved structure, and going back to school meant getting back into a routine. I also loved the idea of new and fresh – a new box of crayons, a fresh start with classmates, an opportunity to study new subjects and read harder books. I was also excited to meet my teacher. Usually, my sister had the same teacher two years before me, and I was excited to create my own experience.

Going back to school meant seeing my friends again. Unlike my current suburban life, we didn't live on a cul-de-sac and have play dates. During the summer, especially before I could drive, seeing my friends was usually limited to 4-H club meetings, the county fair, and perhaps a birthday party. There was also the promise of new students on the first day of school. In a small town, new students are a big deal. When you spend K-12 with the same 80 kids, anyone new is a potential new friend. My best friend from my small town was a new student on the first day of 3rd grade.

Finding these "first day of school" moments in our adult lives is a perfect way to remember Her. She's there when you can't fall asleep the night before leaving for a big vacation. She's the one who is a mixture of nervous and excited when you take on a new assignment at your place of work or in the community. For me, I remember Her when I have something new or enjoyable happening with my work, or when my kids get to have a fun experience for the first time.

CHAPTER 5

Remembering my Roots

This section wouldn't be complete without filling in the picture of those people who were formative in building Her up. In my case, my grandparents, parents and sister played that role. The only house I ever remember living in, and where my parents still live today, is a yellow ranch-style house with brown shutters and garage door. It's located on two and a half acres, surrounded on the north, east and south by fields that would rotate each year between corn, soybeans and wheat. To the west was my grandparents' house, separated from our land by a pond.

Both of my parents worked full-time and having grandparents next door meant built-in latchkey services. I knew it as "getting off the bus at Grandma and Grandpa's house." Once off the bus, my sister and I were met with an afterschool snack from Grandma. It was usually some flavor of Archway cookies (iced oatmeal was my favorite) and flavored drink mix. We didn't typically stay for dinner, but when we did, it usually included an assortment of boiled foods like potatoes, ham slices and green beans. No matter what was for dinner, there was always angel food cake for dessert. Before mom and dad picked us up, we kept ourselves busy working in Grandpa's shop; I learned how to pound nails and use small power tools in those after-school lessons. Sometimes we crafted with Grandma. Frequently, we played Uno. The most memorable day of Uno was when we heard a giant boom followed by an earthquake-like shake. My sister, grandma and I quickly got under the kitchen table, unsure of what happened. When we realized there were going to be no more booms or shakes, we came out from under the table, only to see that the giant red barn that stood next to the pond had fallen off of its foundation. Thankfully, the barn had long ago been abandoned and no one was hurt, but we will never forget the day the barn fell down.

I learned how to spend quality time with people by watching my grandparents. They had amazing friends who they played cards with and attended civic and community events together. Every year, they pulled their camper to the Seneca County Fairground and oversaw the antique tractor display. They showed me what it was like to be part of the community. My grandfather passed away when I was a senior in college and my grandmother when I was 32. At each of their funerals, we shared laughs and tears with people who knew them both their whole lives.

My parents, who met their senior year in high school, were in the first graduating class of Seneca East High School, which brought together Attica High (my mom's school) and Republic High (my dad's school). My mom, Mary Powell, taught me how to be a strong woman, organizer of anything from a closet to a thousand-person gathering, and most importantly, how to be a mom who raises independent daughters. Here are five of the top lessons I've learned from my mom during my first 40 years.

You can be a great mom, wife, sister, grandmother and friend AND have a career. Mom never missed anything in our lives, but she was quick to give us responsibilities to ease the load she was carrying. Don't get me wrong; she still probably did 70% of the household work, but the to-do list from mom wasn't anything my sister and I would mess with on a summer day or during a latchkey afternoon.

It's possible to work hard, have high expectations AND care about people. My mom cares a whole lot about a whole lot of people. She also doesn't tolerate crap work. Some may call this tough love. I call it the best kind of leader we can ask for.

Rise as opportunities and challenges come to you. My mom does not have a degree from a four-year college. That hasn't stopped her from going after the next job. She started her career as a secretary and ended as a COO. For her, it was all about stepping into the next challenge, figuring out the next problem-solving opportunity, and using her experience to move the needle.

You can complain about something as long as you plan to fix it. Over the years, we saw mom get excited and passionate about things. This passion frequently turned into action and led mom to be a key leader at the local school, church and community organizations. This is why one of my leading management asks is that you can complain about something as long as you are prepared to be part of the solution.

Homemade cookies are the best way to anyone's heart. There isn't much to add to this and cookies will continue to play an important role in this book.

My dad played a similar role in teaching me many lessons throughout life. My dad worked 2nd shift when I was in kindergarten, which meant I was his shadow on the days I wasn't in school. I was his shot-gun passenger in his pick-up truck. There were no strangers on our adventures, whether to the hardware store, grain elevator, post office or bank. We spent many days helping Grandpa on the farm (I mainly remember sweeping up the fine dust that collected on the barn floor.) I also remember being with my dad when the Challenger exploded. I was in kindergarten and it was one of the days when I was not in school. We were going to eat our lunch while we watched the space shuttle launch. For my generation, the Challenger explosion is one of the first formative memories we have, and I can be grateful that I shared it with my dad and wasn't watching along with my classmates. While there are dozens of lessons from my dad, I can boil them all down into the top lesson he's taught me:

It's okay to talk to strangers. In a small town, you get to know people. I observed my dad getting to know people since I was a little girl. Being with my dad taught me that strangers can become acquaintances, who can become friends, who can become lifelong companions. In a digital world, we often feel like we know people, but what we know is only shown through carefully edited photos or cleverly curated words. What I learned from my dad through talking to strangers are things you will never see on Instagram and never fit concisely into a 280 character tweet.

I recall a summer vacation to Maine when we were camping next to another family. In true small town fashion, my dad made sure to introduce himself and our family. While the niceties could have ended there, our families continued the conversation and, by the end of the trip, were sharing addresses. I believe my parents still exchange Christmas cards with that family today.

Dad showed me how to get to know people. I might have been embarrassed at times, or rolled my eyes, but I think of those moments often. When I'm at a networking event and want to hide in the corner or see someone walking toward me and want to turn away, I think to myself, "What would Dave

Powell do?" and I usually end up making a friend out of a stranger or make someone else feel at home in a new place.

I couldn't fully remember my roots without including my sister, Nicci. Sisterhood was as much a part of growing up in rural America as the county fair and country roads. We didn't live on a cul-de-sac with other kids. We didn't have play dates and endless activities. We had each other.

Here is one of our parents' favorite stories to share, which took place when I was 3 or 4, and Nicci was 5 or 6. I was sitting on the toilet before bedtime when she made a comment to me about "being little". My response was to say "me not little" and punch her in the nose. While my parents laugh about it today (and, I'm sure, were holding back their laughter when it happened), they must have made it a teachable moment.

I don't have memories of fighting with my sister. I remember playing teacher, doctor, and dress up. We regularly choreographed gymnastics, dance, jump rope and roller skating routines to the tunes of Paula Abdul and Milli Vanilli. There were endless hours of swinging in our backyard while Chicago's Greatest Hits played on the boombox. In our shared bedroom, we had flashlight wars and talked under the covers when we were supposed to be sleeping.

As we got older, we partnered on 4-H projects and became two-time state fair speaking champions together. We played duets on the piano. We bought our first car together when I was 13 and she was 16. We were together the only time she ever ditched the car, bailed out by small town strangers and our Uncle Bob. We were there for each other when the inevitable high school breakups happened. She hosted me at Baldwin-Wallace when she was in college for both classroom and extracurricular orientation.

Fast forward four decades, two weddings, four apartments, three houses, multiple jobs and four children later and I am still proud of our sisterhood. Not only is my sister a loyal friend and hard worker, but she also has a perspective on the world that many appreciate. I'm most proud of my sister for being a great example to her teenage boys. She's shown them from an early age what inclusion and compassion look like. She shared the following words with them and it's become an inspiration for many beyond her home:

In this house we don't judge people by the color of their skin, who they love or how they worship. AND if I ever hear you say anything to the contrary, you will be grounded for the remainder of your time in this house. AND if I ever hear you say anything to the contrary after you leave this house, you will not be welcome here again. Harsh words for a dark and hateful time. Hate starts somewhere. It stops at home. ~ Nicci Avalon

Remembering Her is also about Remembering Them. The people who have seen us at our best, our worst, and all of the places in between. I wouldn't be Her without Them. For this, I am eternally grateful.

Summary

Remembering Her is about uncovering and recounting. It's blowing an inch of dust off of the actual or proverbial memory box in order to recall the stories, scenes and events that made Her who she was. When we wipe away the dust, we find the song in Her heart. The skip in Her step. The glint in Her eye. The humor in Her voice. When we take time to Remember Her, we have a better chance of Letting Her Out.

Reflection Questions:
Remember Her

- What artifacts or archives can you dig through to Remember Her? Your own diaries or journals? Scrapbooks? Yearbooks? Photo albums? Newspaper clippings? Home videos?

- In the absence of your own archives or diaries, what was happening in the world during your formative years to help you Remember Her? What movies, music and world events can help you remember?

- What do you remember about the Her you see in photos from your childhood? How often is she making an appearance in adulthood?

- What parts of your childhood do you reminisce about the most? What memories will your children never experience because life isn't as it used to be?

- What were your "streaks of happiness" moments that can help you remember Her? How are you actively looking for and appreciating streaks of happiness in our current day-to-day lives?

- How did your ambition show up as a child? Were you on the leaderboard for Girl Scout cookie sales? Did you coordinate ad-hoc community service projects when your neighbors were in need? Where does that ambition show up today? Where is it suppressed today?

- What moments from your younger days can you relive in order to remember Her?

- Who can you talk to or visit with who will help you remember Her? Siblings, family members, friends, teachers?

- What problems were you solving at a young age for pure joy and fun? How are you still solving similar problems today?

- What did you want to be when you grew up that didn't make sense to you at the time? How does it fit into your passion or profession today?

Section 2

RECONNECT
TO HER

Section 2

Reconnect to Her

I've taken many solo drives from my current home in Dublin, Ohio, a suburb of Columbus, to my childhood home in Republic, Ohio while writing this book. There is something about leaving the cul-de-sac life and emerging onto open, 2-lane roads surrounded on both sides by fields of corn, wheat, and soybeans, under a clear-blue sky filled with billowy clouds that allows me to Reconnect to Her. During those 90-minute journeys, I can feel Her emerging. Traveling the roads where I found freedom as a teenager not only floods my mind with memories, but also brings back the excitement of driving my old Buick Century to the next adventure that awaited me.

If Remembering Her was about blowing the dust off of photo albums and memory boxes in order to recall the stories, relationships, and life-shaping events that made you who you are today, reconnecting is about bringing those memories into your bones. When we reconnect to Her, we feel the feelings she felt. We smile her smile. We cry her tears. We stand in those moments that will forever be frozen in time. We remind both our body and our mind that somewhere, perhaps deep in the recesses of our memory or perhaps lingering on the surface, she is there. Before you can Let Her Out, I invite you to reconnect to her as she was at the age of eight, 15 or 20.

If Remembering Her was about blowing the dust off of photo albums and memory boxes in order to recall the stories, relationships, and life-shaping events that made you who you are today, reconnecting is about bringing those memories into your bones.

The treasure trove of diaries, essays, and pictures made it easy to remember Her. Pictures and words put people, places and events at the front and center of my mind. This doesn't mean it paved a smooth path to reconnect to Her. It was hard to remind myself of the quickly formed opinions, strong judgements, jealous friendships, and broken hearts that seemed to be par for the course in my younger days. Although those things shaped Her, time and age haven't made the reconnection easier.

There is low hanging fruit when it comes to reconnecting. Baby pictures and senior portraits that line the halls of your childhood home, family vacation memories that surface each year when adventure awaits, and the feelings of nostalgia you get when you see the marching band or football team take the field bring forth memories and emotions on demand. These are likely the memories that are sitting on the surface and are the ones you reconnect to most often.

In this step of the journey, I'm inviting you to reconnect at a deeper level. In order for me to reconnect, I had to go past the teenage breakups, family and friendship drama, and even the awards and recognition that came from being a high-achieving kid. I had to reconnect to the girl who had big dreams and even bigger plans. To the girl who wanted to be President of the United States of America. To the girl who knew that she had something to offer to the world. It's this girl who can change the world. That's why we need to reconnect to Her so badly. If there are a million girls in the world with big dreams, but who let life dim those plans, we are leaving potential and promise on the table.

If there are a million girls in the world with big dreams, but who let life dim those plans, we are leaving potential and promise on the table.

Whether your dream is to build a life in your hometown or to venture to far-flung places, if you live your life as fully as you feel when you reconnect to Her, you will be unstoppable.

In order to inspire your memories, here are four areas I've decided are worth reconnecting to on my quest to Let Her Out.

CHAPTER 6

Reconnecting to my voice

When I was eight, I joined the Scipio Shamrocks, the local 4-H Club. 4-H is a youth leadership and development program, typically found in rural and agricultural areas, where kids learn hands-on skills like raising animals, woodworking, cooking and sewing. I didn't live on a working farm, so I took domestic projects and learned skills like sewing, cooking, first aid, and my game-changer: public speaking. My first summer in 4-H, I went to a workshop to learn about the "demonstration contest". This is where you pick something to teach an audience and then demonstrate it to them. I chose to teach the audience how to make oatmeal cookies. I spent the first month of the summer practicing my presentation, which meant my family ate A LOT of oatmeal cookies. I titled my demonstration, "What's the Deal with Oatmeal". On the day I gave my presentation, I packed up my mom's mixer and all of my supplies and set up in a dusty building at the county fairground. I was pleased with my performance. My practice paid off and I received a passing grade. I didn't win any awards, but that was okay for me. I was a kid having fun over my summer vacation.

Later that day, when I was visiting my best friend in the cow barn, someone in my 4-H club said, "Congratulations on qualifying for the State Fair." Neither I, nor my parents, knew what they were talking about. Apparently, the top 10 scores got to represent the county at the State Fair. I was number 10.

A couple of weeks later, I packed up the same mixer and ingredients and headed to the State Fair in Columbus, Ohio. We had no idea how the process worked, so my parents and I showed up early in the morning and I sat on a cooler filled with oatmeal cookie ingredients for what seemed like hours, waiting to take my turn. I was wearing a light blue apron with tiny pink, yellow and green hearts with 'Natalie' embroidered in yellow on the front. I stared at my skinned-up knees and church shoes, hoping this focus would make the time go faster. As I sat there, I saw kids who were clearly pros at the 4-H demonstration. They had professionally printed posters. They had snazzy props. They came out to intro music and handled the microphone like television hosts ready for the next round of a game show. I had 50 cent poster boards from the drug store, decorated with a Crayola marker. Mercifully, my turn came. I was equally relieved when I was finished, both because I did my best just like I did at the county fair, and because it meant I could get away from the professional kids surrounding me. When I re-packed the cooler, folded up the apron, and wiped down the mixer, the fair volunteers told my family and me to make sure we came back at the end of the day for the awards ceremony. I didn't see the point because I wasn't going to win. I saw what my competition was like and figured, since they had it all figured out, they would take home the prizes.

My parents, being the wise ones on this amateur journey, ensured that we came back. As the award ceremony started, I was shocked when they called my name. I won. I won an honorable mention, which came in the form of a purple ribbon. I cradled that purple ribbon all the way home. Someone saw something in me. They recognized my talent. That was the best day of my life. That purple ribbon hung on my wall until I went off to college and my mom redecorated my room. I was proud of what I had done. My work was my own. My handmade poster boards were fine.

That was the day I found my voice. I, the knobby-kneed brown-haired girl from Republic, Ohio, felt for the first time what it was like to be handed the microphone and hear her voice amplified over the sound system.

Public speaking became my passion and my sport. Over the next ten years, I became one of those "pro" speakers with snazzy props and carefully designed posters. It seemed like I always had something to say. It seemed like people were always willing to listen. When I spoke, I experienced flow. Everything around me blurred and I was able to move through the experience with ease and joy.

The 4-H speaking turned into standing at the church pulpit. I regularly attended the regional meetings of the United Church of Christ. It was there I learned about something called the "Speak Out." All that was required was to sign up for a one-minute time slot and take the microphone at the appointed time. Many people used this time to advertise their artisan crafts available in the fellowship hall. I took the microphone like I was the closing speaker in a packed convention center. Here are two of my early speak-outs:

May 6, 1995 (age 15) - 1 Timothy 4:12 - Do not let anyone look down on you because you are young, but be an example for the believers in your speech, your conduct, your love, faith and purity.

Out of everyone sitting here today, not everyone has been to a foreign country, nor has everyone seen the seven wonders of the world, but one thing everyone has experienced is youth.

Being a youth in 1995 is different from the youth of the '40s, '50s, '60s and '70s. One of the most common phrases I hear is, "When I was young..." I hope everyone has begun to realize that our world is changing, and not so much for the better.

I hope you can see that the youth of today face many problems. I also hope you realize that there are solutions to these problems.

So I ask that you welcome the youth with open arms into your church. If the world isn't fit for children of today, hopefully it will be fit for their children and grandchildren. We aren't the future. We are the present. With all generations working together, hopefully the world will be fit for the elderly, the middle aged, the adolescents, and most of all, the children!

April 1997 (age 17) - "Do you know that only 3% of our nation has 'the edge'?" Before I tell you what 'the edge' is, I'd like everyone to shut your eyes and think about something you would like to have, do, or achieve. At some point today, write down what you visualized. You now have the edge.

Set goals, don't visualize them in your head and dream about them at night. Write them on paper and read them daily. Once you have written them down, evaluate your list of goals. Simply assessing your list will trigger new ideas, alternative solutions and more goals.

With these goals, make a difference in your own life. You ultimately determine how far you will go. In the books of Matthew and Luke it says 'ask and you will receive, seek and you will find, knock and the door will be opened to you.' I'd add one more – set goals and you will overcome obstacles, jump hurdles, and you will be a success!"

At the ages of 15 and 17, I knew my words were powerful. It was written by public speaking competition judges on their scoresheets. I heard it from the adults who approached me after I gave a speech to tell me how proud and appreciative they were to hear my words. Most of all, I could feel it in my heart and body after I put the microphone back in its holder and exited the stage.

I was a girl from a small town with big ideas and I wasn't afraid to step in front of a microphone. I don't know where I got my inspiration, but it flowed freely and often during my youth. Reading my words again while writing this book gives me chills. This is the way I want to reconnect to bring Her forward.

The other place that has informed this reconnecting are those many diary entries where I was able to reflect on the words and the ovation. Here are a few:

May 7, 1995 (age 15): I think I might have found my calling. I did a speak out on my view of a world fit for children. It came from my heart and it touched so many people. I loved the feeling of hearing my words echo throughout the church. It was indescribable. I then read it in church this morning...maybe minister is in my future. I know that whatever path I choose I will find my way.

June 7, 1995 (age 15): I might get an actual chance to deliver a sermon. A local pastor was so impressed by my speak out that he wants me to come to his church to speak. I just think that my speak out was a sign. Something that came from my heart touched many people. Maybe that will be my life?

March 29, 1997 (age 17): I gave my speech again. I needed the renewal of its message. I am becoming mentally and socially more rounded as my physical state remains well. That speech has given me so much. A sense of knowledge, a basis for my life's rituals, a public awareness.

June 19, 1997 (age 17): I got a chance to take the microphone yesterday. Among negative comments and lecturing statements, I assured my peers with a thought. When there is hope for the future, there is power in the present. Therefore, where there is hope, there is power. I didn't expect the reaction I got. Teenagers normally let things pass by when they are spoken word - but not the 600 youth in Washington DC. The roof felt as if it was being raised. I added a positive note. So goes the story of my life.

This voice, this conviction, is how I'm happy to reconnect to Her. She took the microphone without hesitation, wrote inspiring speeches on the back of a church bulletin, and didn't let peer pressure push her into a corner. Reconnecting to the words I wrote allowed me to think closely about why finding my voice was so important to me, both as a child and adult. I was keenly observant of the world around me. I noticed when the same person was always picked last for the dodgeball team. I felt terrible for the kid who had trouble forming words when asked to speak out loud in front of the class. I recognized when my peers turned to alcohol and sex to help them cope with life. It felt both safe and powerful for me to pick up a microphone or pen and encourage them to persevere. Standing on a stage or authoring the next essay felt like a safe way to show I cared. I also needed to hear the messages for myself. As articulate and confident as I was, I still needed a cheerleader to tell me I was kind and good and smart. While the context of the words I use has shifted since I was in that dusty barn as an eight-year-old, Reconnecting to Her reminds me of the broader mission to use my voice to motivate and inspire those who need it the most.

Pause & Reflect:
Reconnecting to Your Voice

- How do you define the voice of your youth? Even if you didn't take the microphone or win any purple ribbons, you had moments when your voice was strong, your ideas were clear, and you felt like you were on top of the world. What were those moments?

- What can you find to remind you of your voice from your youth? Do you have a box of middle and high school essays that can connect you to the sage (or silly) things you said in your youth? Do you have a digitized copy of your early public speaking performances?

CHAPTER 7

Reconnecting to my strength

I'm standing with my toe barely an inch away from the painted black line on the shiny gym floor at the school gym in Republic, Ohio. It was a line I'd hovered over hundreds of times as a rock-star volleyball player during junior high. It was the line where I practiced in order to serve a perfect 15-0 game on the opposing team's turf only a year before. On this day, everything hinged on the overhand serve I'd been perfecting all summer long. Every day, I practiced serving over the net in my backyard next to the cornfield. I worked so hard at volleyball camp that my knees were scabbed and my hands were swollen. I silently hoped to be handed one of the softer balls in order to have more leverage on the serve. (This is well before Tom Brady's deflate gate scandal during Superbowl XLIX.) One serve over. Phew. Another one clears the net. And a miss. And another miss. A final serve barely clears the net.

It was going to be a tricky decision. I was a starting volleyball player all throughout 7th and 8th grade. Going into the summer before my freshman year in high school, I thought I was a shoe-in for the team. As the summer wore on, so did my confidence. Here's what I said about it in my diary:

> *July 14, 1994 (age 14) Volleyball camp. Excruciating. My knees are so sore, not to mention the rest of my body. I have no clue if I will make the team. I really want to be on the team, but there is this part of me who really doesn't want to be on the team.*

As a junior high student, I did what many small town kids do and played three sports. I was on the volleyball, basketball and track teams. I had my moments of glory on the court and on the field, like that perfect 15-0 volleyball game, and the time I was substituted last minute into the 4x100 relay team at the district track meet and we took home first place. Those literal and figurative ribbons hung on my wall in my pink-heart wallpapered bedroom. Up to that point in life, I was always on the team and wanted to believe with my whole heart that it wouldn't be different this time.

Finally, the time came when the coach called me – and only me – into the entryway of the gym. This is the space I entered every day for the past nine years to go to my elementary and junior high school classrooms. It's where I purchased my lunch tickets before school. It's where I went when I needed a break during junior high school dances. There, in that space where I formed so many memories, another one was going to be added to the list. Coach told me that I wasn't going to be on the team. I was the only girl who didn't make the cut. I remember staring at her numbly. I wanted to be strong and show that I wasn't disappointed. That strength only held up for a few minutes and I dissolved into a puddle of tears.

After I gathered my things and pulled myself together, my neighbor Linda picked me up from the tryout. She saw that I was upset and we promptly went back to her house and she did what any good small town mom would do and made me a huge ice cream sundae. She reassured me that things were going to be ok.

Even though I deflected the pain, not making that team hurt. The only sport I continued with in 9th grade was track. Early in track practice I reveled at how good it felt to run. Of one experience at practice, I said, *"I like the feeling of being out of breath knowing that I just did something good for my body - Hopefully my running will pay off this track season."* I'd like to tell you that there were other championship runs around the track, but there weren't. Most track practices during freshman year went something like this: Change for practice. Run obligatory two lap warm up around the track. Take off for "long run" through town with friend and teammate, Jackie. Arrive at her brother's house approximately 800 yards later. Turn on TV. Watch the Ricki Lake Show. Eat Oreo cookies. Return to the locker room appearing exhausted from that long run.

After I was cut from the volleyball team and watched my track gold dreams go up in smoke with the Oreos and salacious talk show TV, I knew I had to do some form of exercise to keep in shape. I knew how good it felt to be strong and lean. With formalized team sports off the table, I had an opportunity to figure out how to pave my own path toward health and fitness in a time and place where it wasn't a regular part of life.

I went to the local YMCA for a while, but that was 20 minutes away and required a licensed driver. Country roads weren't conducive to running or other distance activities. Crossfit, Orangetheory, and all of the other fitness crazes we've seen hit the market didn't exist in Republic, Ohio. Therefore, I utilized the resources available to me and assembled a workout station in our partially finished basement. I had a step for step aerobics and a few dumbbells.

I went to the local library and scoured the shelves for workout videos. I found every step aerobic, cardio, and resistance training video I could find. Against all copyright laws, I dubbed the library copies and created my own "mix-tape" of workout videos. Each morning before school, I would complete one of the workouts. During that 4-year period, I got to know Jane Fonda, Karen Voight, Gin Miller and the dancers from MTVs "The Grind" workout. This was my time to feel powerful and stay in shape on my own terms. After a few months of this routine, I was as fit as any of the 3-sport varsity athletes in my school.

I've carried the memories of being cut from the team and making my own path toward fitness throughout my life. While my workout routine has shifted as I've gone through different phases of life (stay tuned for more on this in later chapters), the workout-in-the-basement-to-videos morning routine is something that has stuck. Today, the main difference is that I don't have to rewind the VCR tapes (and that I legally purchased all of the programs I use.) My current workout companions are a variety of Beachbody and YouTube fitness stars, who might not rock the aerobic leotards like the workout stars of the 90s, but they motivate me to continue staying fit on my own terms.

I could have thrown in the towel on fitness after being cut from the volleyball team. I could have stuck to the daily activity in gym class, but I appreciated at a young age that physical fitness is extremely important for emotional and psychological well being. When my alarm clock rings at 6:15 a.m., all I need to do is reconnect to Her and how she built her strength and resilience. Reconnecting to the Her that avoided the snooze button makes it easier to get up, tie my shoes and hit play on the workout. If I could marshal resources in order to build my own home gym, complete with routines from the 90s' best fitness leaders, as a 15-year old small town girl, nothing should stand in my way with the resources available today.

Pause & Reflect:
Reconnecting to Your Strength

- How do you remember Her physical strength? What about Her mental strength?

- What teams were you on that help you reconnect to Her?

- What teams were you cut from or didn't dare try out for and how did that shape Her?

- What is a moment when you took control of your strength and your body?

CHAPTER 8

Reconnecting to Young Love

Why did I start that diary in 1988? Because I liked a boy. Why did I keep writing all of those years? Usually, because I liked a boy. I thanked one boy in my journal for being in my life simply so I'd pick up the pen. There is one love that was hard to remember, but I will never forget. It's the type of love we need to connect to as we continue to love, fear love, and step toward love throughout our life.

It all began during the fall of 2nd grade. My first crush.

December 27, 1988 (age 8 - my first diary entry ever) - I want to go back to school for 2 reasons - 1. I want to see my best friend. 2. I want to go back because I have a crush on a boy. I AM NOT GOING TO TELL WHO HE IS.

The crush turned into puppy love. We passed letters during class, but per the code of 2nd grade romance, never, ever made eye contact with one another. The romance prepares for the first test: summer vacation.

June 7, 1989 (age 9) - My best friend gave him a letter. It asked if he still liked me. His answer was "yes" so he wrote me and said he might write to me over the summer and I might call him up.

The summer passed. We continued to "go together" during third grade. By fourth grade, we started to become real friends, which meant our elementary school romance was over. In fifth and sixth grade, we were the type of friends who talked to one another, helped each other with math problems, and occasionally shot hoops together in the gym during recess. He was like this with everyone. Then this:

December 17, 1991 (age 11): So much has happened in the past month. This day a month ago, Andy, the one I told you all about, died. He was the boy I have always liked best! He had a heart attack and had to be life flighted to Columbus. It came as a shock to everybody. Since that day, all the 6th graders at Republic have had the roughest time ever. I am so ??? I don't even know what I feel like. For one thing, I didn't go to his funeral. I got sick. And I didn't go to his viewing either. No one understands just how we feel.

The death of Andy, the boy who inspired so many of the early scribbles in the Hello Kitty diary, was a tragic loss to our entire community. He was your typical All-American boy. He loved baseball, was a whiz at math, and was a genuine and kind-hearted kid. Even as time went on, and along with it, more pre-teen and teenage crushes than I remembered, Andy had a hold on my heart.

Fast forward to July 16, 1995 (age 15): I'm crying right now. I just read my diary from 3rd-8th grade. I can't believe the things that happened then. A lot of the diary was about Andy. I never appreciated how much I cared for him. The hardest part to take was when I told about Andy's death. I was so confused then. I still am. I don't know if I should still be grieving. I guess I really never got to grieve.

I think I've learned a lot about love. I know that love at first sight doesn't work. And I know that long distance love doesn't work. I do know that love can look you straight in the face and you can touch it, but aren't quite sure why it's there. I also know that love is supporting your best friend through the biggest transition in her life and your own life. Sometimes I wonder what the next 15 years of my life are going to be like. I know that I'll look back at this diary some day and laugh, but for now this is the only life I know and the only life I've got to live, so I'm treating it like a serious matter.

May 15, 1997 (age 17): Tomorrow is Memorial Day. It is a time for me to remember people like Andy. He is a veteran to me. A veteran to my world. I wonder often what Andy would be like today. His little brother will enter high school next year. Andy never made it that far. Some survive. Some don't. All are remembered

This love, this boy, is one of the reasons I picked up a pen at the tender age of eight. Even at that young age, I knew that there was power in love and power in human connection. Back then, I called it a crush or a fling or someone to "go with". Now I know that as love.

Whether you reconnect to young love, old love or rekindled love, it's a part of your story. Love continued to be a part of my story throughout my diaries. In junior high alone, I claimed to be in love four times. In high school, I had long-term love and long-distance romance.

Love came hard and fast and ended slow and painful for most of my young life. Many of the people I claimed to love never knew I loved them, because I never told them. I told my diary and I told my best friend, but I never told them.

Reading about crushes and young love made me cringe. It also made me feel like I haven't felt in a long time. It's been tough to reconnect to the Her that fell in love, loved hard and got hurt harder. It was also the most enlightening part because it reminded me what it was like to feel with my whole body and soul. When you love someone at the age of 15, the sun, moon and stars orbit around that person. When they kiss you in the moonlight, you remember it for the rest of your life. When they break up with you over email, you feel pain like you've never felt before.

When you love someone at the age of 15, the sun, moon and stars orbit around that person.

I continued to write about love in all of those diaries. During my reconnecting, I closely read all of the pages from 1998-2001. 1998 is the year I rekindled a long-distance romance that I thought could end in marriage. I said it often on those pages, and as I re-read those pages in order to write this one,

I shook my head. The relationship eventually turned tense and cold in a way that makes me shiver to this day. It's a relationship that I went to my freshman Resident Advisor to for advice on numerous occasions. His advice was always the same: dump him. I've now been married to that Resident Advisor, Rob, for 18 years.

What I realized in the reconnecting was that all of the love I experienced prior to my relationship with Rob was an "all or nothing" kind of love. I was never friends with those boys first. We went from zero to dating in a blink of an eye. With Rob, friendship came first, then love. The day I went into his room for the first time, I knew there could be something more than friendship in our future. Even though he was a sports-loving engineer, his bookshelf was lined with the same inspirational books and music as mine. Late in my freshman year of college, I had this to say:

February 12, 1999 (age 19): I'm falling for RA Rob. He's sensitive, successful, smart, a great listener, a good friend. And he has been from day 1. From saga to saga. From breakup to reunion to breaking up again. I don't know whether it's because it's forbidden, or if it's just because we understand each other. Maybe it's all rolled into one.

June 9, 1999 (age 19): Somewhere along the line, I started hanging out in room 2357 of Lincoln Tower. Here resides the most intelligent, in-spirational, spiritual, strong, sweet, intimate, humorous, brave and true person I have ever met. I want to be with Rob. I don't need to be with him. I want to hold his hand. I want to do his dishes [SIDE NOTE: oh boy, there have been a lot of dishes]. I want to keep making little discoveries with him. I am so in love with this boy. If this is what love is like - I'm in it forever!

Rob and I spent his senior year at The Ohio State University dreaming about the future. In some of those dreams, he was in Boston at MIT and I was in Washington DC in law school. In others, he was at Stanford or Berkeley while I made waves in the non-profit scene on the West Coast. Rob ended up at Stanford to earn his PhD and proposed along the banks of Mirror Lake on the Ohio State campus during Homecoming Weekend my senior year. We thought about continuing on our separate paths once I graduated, but it didn't seem to make any sense to be apart when we had been separated by 2,000 miles for two years. We had a Labor Day weekend wedding in 2002 and began our married life together in Palo Alto, California (more on that later.)

This friendship turned love turned life partnership helped me understand how I let love into my life. I have a slow and steady approach to building and maintaining relationships, whether with friends, family, service or vocation. Reconnecting to love this way brings even more love into my life.

How does thinking about young love make you feel? Are you cringing thinking about your first love? Is your breath a little shallower thinking about long lost love? Reconnecting to Her is as much about the love as it is the pain. Whether you've been married 25 years or are still a newlywed, are waiting for the love of your life, or are with your first love, reconnecting to how she loved is a crucial step in letting her out. The memories that come forward might be kept between you, your diary and God, or they may be the stuff of memoirs and romance novels. Reconnect to the Her who loved with her whole heart. The biggest lesson you can take from this is that you don't have to settle for anything less than a whole heart experience. Whether the focus of your love is romantic, in friendship, with family or through vocation and service, you deserve unconditional love.

Pause & Reflect: Reconnecting to Young Love

- How do you remember young love?

- What prom photos or love notes do you need to pull out of storage to connect to long-ago-love?

- Who stole your heart only to have you take it back?

- Who still holds a piece of your heart in theirs?

- How did you experience other types of love, like love for friends, family, and community, in your youth? How did that shape you?

CHAPTER 9

Reconnecting to Conviction

When I was eight, my parents gave me a button that said, "I'm not opinionated, I'm just always right." Apparently, I came out of the womb with thoughts and feelings and I was never afraid to share them. The combination of this natural-born trait with a small town upbringing meant that I saw what conviction and passion do in a community. One of the strongest memories I have about conviction as an adolescent was witnessing my community come together to ensure that the Seneca East School District levy passed.

I was an 8th grader and everything I had been hoping for out of my high school experience was on the line because of the levy. If the levy failed, there would be no band, athletics would be pay-to-play, and a number of other reductions would send my high school dreams up in smoke.

For months leading up to election day, the parents of our community rallied. They had tough conversations with people whose kids were grown and didn't have a vested interest in the schools anymore. They talked at public forums about the opportunities we would miss if the appropriate funding wasn't available.

Students got involved, too. We made and put out levy signs. I remember a few conversations I had with people on the fence, mostly empty nesters. I had them tell me about memories they had of their kids when they were in high school. They would tell me about their son who played on the football team or their daughter who was in the school musical. I begged them not to take that away from us – from me.

The night before the election, I prayed that the levy would pass. I visualized myself on the football field playing in the marching band. Running track. On stage in the school musical. And I prayed that the hard work and the case the community made for its children would lead to victory.

The levy passed. I don't remember by how much – it might have been a landslide, and it might have been a close call. All that mattered to me was that I would get to continue on the path that I had been dreaming about.

This taught me that things worth fighting for are worth having a conversation about. There was no social media or internet to rely on when the levy was on the ballot. We had to talk directly to voters about the implications of their vote for our community. I never took the experiences I had in school for granted, knowing how hard the community worked to ensure I had the opportunities I did.

I was never short of conviction and passion, and my feelings about justice and equality appeared early in life. As a fifteen year old, I had this to say about the Oklahoma City Bombing: *I think today I felt what real anger is about. On Wednesday, Oklahoma City was bombed and 400 people are dead, injured or missing...I guess I don't know why anyone would kill so many people. I don't understand when people learn to hate. You aren't born prejudiced. You have to learn it, but who would ever teach hate?*

Ohio State became a place for my conviction and passion to take root. I was a resident advisor (RA) during my sophomore and junior years. In my second year, I had a co-RA, Tony, who managed the boys' side of the hall. One day, Tony came into my room and asked if we could talk. He then proceeded to tell me that he was gay. I was grateful that he told me and offered to support him in any way as he continued his coming out journey.

Later that quarter, we had our weekly staff meeting and the mandatory discussion topic was LGBT awareness. Our hall director read through a hypothetical situation about a fictional student who was struggling with his sexual orientation. The entire time he was reading this made-up scenario, I was thinking of Tony. Tony was raised in a small town and finally had the courage to come out during his time in college. In an uncharacteristic way, I interrupted my hall director and said, "Wouldn't this be more meaningful if we could ask Tony how he feels?"

Tony looked at me with wide eyes. I assumed he was out to the rest of the staff, but, apparently, I was still part of his inner circle. After the commotion died down and wide eyes returned to normal (and Tony gave me a look that suggested it was okay that I outed him), I cried. I cried for Tony that night in front of my staff members. I cried for someone who didn't feel like he could be his true self in front of us. I cried that we felt it more important as a staff to work through fictional scenarios than to hear directly from someone who was living this as his truth. I cried out of anger. I cried out of frustration.

That moment served as an important lesson for me in how I take a stand on issues. If I cannot put myself in someone's shoes, then I do not deserve to take a stand on an issue that affects them. It's very easy to say you are pro-this and anti-that. But once you put a name, face and story with someone who holds opposing views, you might have a change of heart.

Dialogue around LGBT issues was not part of my small town upbringing, but it was as natural for me to be angry and frustrated for Tony as anyone who had the potential to live a big life, but didn't think he could be fully himself. At the time, I viewed my conviction as an extension of the golden rule. I took time to put myself in other people's shoes on a regular basis. When this wasn't possible because our differences were too great, I tried to garner as much empathy and compassion as possible. The evolution I've experienced over time is to follow the platinum rule. The golden rule is to treat others how you would like to be treated. The platinum rule is to treat other people how *they* want to be treated. In order to do this, we have to understand that we will never be able to fully identify with someone else's experience.

I cannot know what the oppression of homophobia, systemic racism, and poverty feel like because I have never experienced those things, but I can look every person who I meet in the eye, treat them with the respect they deserve, and most importantly, listen to their story.

Everyone has a story that deserves to be heard. By opening ourselves to the stories of others, we open our minds to broader ways of thinking. If we could all take a minute to care about what the person next to us is going through, then we probably wouldn't be so divided as a society.

Everyone has a story that deserves to be heard. By opening ourselves to the stories of others, we open our minds to broader ways of thinking.

My parents likely had no idea what they started when they gave me that "I'm not opinionated, I'm just always right" button when I was eight. Now I know they are glad we can reconnect to Her this way.

Pause & Reflect: Reconnecting to Your Conviction

- What are the earliest beliefs that you remember? How were they formed? How have they evolved?

- How did you decide your positions on controversial issues? How have these positions been challenged, or even changed, over the years?

- What has been your journey walking in other people's shoes?

CHAPTER 10

Reconnecting to Passion

While I will always remember the silence that met me after my solo in *Fiddler on the Roof*, reconnecting to what was happening behind the scenes has been an equally important part of this journey. Because our school was so small, musical participants crossed the boundaries of cliques and groups. There were athletes and farm kids and quiz bowl kids and band kids. Because of this, most of the school was aware of the production and came out to support the show. That's why the following memory still makes my heart jump to my throat.

One day, while the student body was standing in the hallway after lunch waiting for the bell to ring, at which point people take off like it's the starting line of the Boston Marathon, one of my classmates casually, without thought, ripped the poster promoting *Fiddler on the Roof* off of the wall and crumpled it in his hands. I was standing right beside him and was dumbfounded. This is a kid I grew up with my whole life and he was always very nice. I was usually (and still am) one of the most even-mannered, cool headed people around. Not in that moment. I unleashed on him. I screamed. I cried. Before I knew it, we were both in the principal's office. Me, so I could cool off; him, likely to get a talking-to, as later that period he issued a formal apology to me.

Reconnecting to this memory has been a reminder to never rip someone else's poster down. Even though it only took a second for the poster to come down, time stood still. I saw the hours of practice, energy and emotion it took a group of teenagers to build a production about oppression and revolution thrown in a heap on the floor. In that moment, someone disrespected something I held closely to me and I stood in my truth and told him how he hurt me. You might be thinking, "It was a silly poster promoting a silly show." Not to me, not in that moment.

We can't casually cast aside what someone else holds dear or cast judgement on the values, aspirations, and passions of others. My high school classmate might not have thought twice about what he did that day if I wasn't standing right beside him calling him out on it.

We can't casually cast aside what someone else holds dear or cast judgement on the values, aspirations, and passions of others.

The Her that was present that day was the one who was willing to get fired up for something she believed in. An alternative version of her could have let it go, laughed along, or silently seethed all the way to my next class; I'm pretty sure that's what the adult Her would have done. That's why I like reconnecting to this version of Her. All too often, we watch silently as someone rips ours or someone else's poster down because it keeps us comfortable and makes life easy. Let's remember the Her inside of us who stands up for her beliefs and is willing to make a trip to the principal's office if required. Let's also grow in empathy for the person doing the ripping. There are inner battles raging inside everyone that lead to split-second decisions. Sometimes we are on the poster and sometimes we are the one tearing it down. Recognizing our passion and respecting the other side is a balance that most adults find challenging. We can learn from the Her who wants to know more and is willing to walk side-by-side to the principal's office with her opponent.

Summary

Reconnecting to Her is more than looking at pictures and reading her words. It's about bringing ourselves back to the moments when she was living for each moment and owning her ambition. It's feeling in our body what she felt like behind the wheel of a car for the first time, when she failed the test, when she aced the test, and when she fell in love for the first time.

Reflection Questions:
Reconnect to Her

- What brought you joy as a child, teenager and young adult? What activity, relationship or cause made you light up a room? Write those things down in as much detail as you can. Who were you with? What was the scene?

- What 5 adjectives would you use to describe Her?

- What personality traits and characteristics do only your closest childhood friends and family members know about?

- What stories formed your early years? What were the stories of triumph? Of tragedy? Of silliness and glee? Of normal, every-day occurrences that remind you of a simpler time?

- What have you purposely tried to forget? What opportunity do you have to reconnect instead of forget? What opportunity do you have to remember instead of forget?

Intermission

WRITE YOUR STORY

Write Your Story

STOP: Before you proceed, don't skip this step. I know I haven't finished my story yet, but before we move on to the final sections, I invite you to take 20 minutes to complete a powerful exercise that will allow you to write your own story, which will help you further remember and reconnect to Her. (Download the Intermission Template at letherout.com/resources.) More importantly, it will set the stage for the final two sections of the book, where you will be asked to recognize and remove the barriers in order to Let Her Out. Revisiting your own story as follows is a compelling way to identify what's getting in your way before you start the next chapter.

Don't be nervous, thinking you have to write a 40,000-word manifesto. Your story could take the form of bullets on a page, drawings on a coloring sheet, or a typed-out narrative.

I've done variations of this exercise with creativity expert, Artie Isaac; founder of Imprint Coaching & Consulting, Michelle Hollingshead (aka my original coach); and founder of Positive Intelligence, Shirzad Chamine. This is how I combine all of their brilliance in order to help you Let Her Out.

Step 1: Break your life into time blocks. There are a few different ways you can do this:

- Separate your life into five-year increments (0-5; 6-10; 11-15, etc.)

- Divide your life into 5 pieces, so in my case, at age 40: 0-8; 9-16; 17-24; 25-32; 33-40

- Break your life into chapters based on significant life events, years in school, or places you lived

Step 2: Within each time block, describe the following:

- What is the single adjective you'd use to describe yourself?

- What activity had the greatest meaning for you?

- Which relationships were most important?

- What were your greatest accomplishments or achievements?

- What were your biggest challenges and obstacles?

- What did this period of your life teach you?

Step 3: Step back and review your story.

- Circle or highlight the words that embody Her. Is there a difference between the words you selected now versus the words she would have picked then?

- Of all the experiences, which were the most defining?

Step 4: Create a summary statement or Let Her Out mantra.

- Based on where you have been, write in *one sentence* who she is and how you want Her to show up in the world.

- Be creative, make it pretty, draw a picture. Whatever it takes to make this meaningful.

- Post this somewhere you can see it frequently. Print it and hang it over your mirror or on your desk. Make it the wallpaper on your phone. At the very least, use it as your bookmark as you finish reading Let Her Out.

Step 5: Share your story and mantra.

- Share your story and mantra with a friend, partner, or family member. Your story deserves to be heard and there is no better place to start than with someone you trust and love.

Section 3

RECOGNIZE AND REMOVE BARRIERS TO HER

Recognize and Remove the Barriers to Her

Now that you've written (or sketched or doodled) your own life story, I hope you can see how she is still a big part of you. If she's been with us all along, it begs the question: where did she go? Does she simply vanish overnight without as much as a goodbye or farewell? Does she slowly back out of the room so as to not be noticed? I've come to the conclusion that what happens over time is that she erects barriers, both consciously and subconsciously, that keep Her in instead of letting Her out. From the work I do with my coaching clients, as well as the personal work I've done with my own coaches, I've identified two types of barriers that get built throughout our lives.

First, there are external barriers, including time, money, family commitments, job responsibilities, and lack of access to the things we enjoyed doing when we were younger. These are my favorite types of barriers to discuss in a coaching conversation, because, typically, where there is a will, there is a way to remove them.

Second are internal barriers. These are built on the feelings of shame, guilt, and "not-enoughness" that almost every woman I know carries around with her. Some carry it in a tiny, designer handbag. Others drag it behind them like a load of luggage meant for a six-month sabbatical. This is much harder to work through and is where we will spend most of our time and energy in this section - and, quite frankly, in our lives.

In this section, I will help you recognize and remove the barriers you've built that are keeping Her in. I will start by describing and working through external barriers and move to internal barriers. I will ask questions I have found success with in my coaching practice to help clients overcome the oftentimes self-imposed barriers to Her.

I mentioned this at the beginning of the book and it's important enough to repeat again: If you have experienced significant trauma in your life, make sure you are walking through this section with the appropriate care. I have not experienced, nor will reflect on, any significant personal trauma, but for you, these stories and exercises could stir up memories from the way-back machine that are best suited to discuss with a therapist or trained mental health professional.

CHAPTER 11

Removing External Barriers

Time. Money. Obligations. Yes. Yes. Yes. All day long, these real, tangible barriers get in the way of us experiencing HER as she could be experienced.

Think critically about your responses throughout the first two sections of the book. What activities, experiences, and relationships lit you up? Who did you spend time with? What made you, you? Now, identify the external barriers that are standing in the way of your enjoying these things today. What is keeping Her in instead of letting Her out? I'll give you a list of thought starters:

- Time
- Money
- Schedule
- Forgot How
- Lack of Access to materials or equipment
- Other Duties As Assigned

I built an external barrier in early adulthood that serves as a great example of how to push through this type of block. The barrier was to music, something that you already know by reading halfway through this book, has been a cornerstone in my life. After graduating from high school and moving away from my small town, the pianos, sheet music and choir practices disappeared from my life. Away went my private living room concerts and jam sessions. After not making it into The Best Damn Band in the Land at Ohio State, I decided I didn't want music to be part of my college experience. As a result, music slowly left my life just as I left my small town.

The first barrier I erected was not having access to the right materials; in my case, a piano. The piano was the place where the connection to songs, improvisation and emotion through music was born. While living in tiny one-bedroom apartments, a piano seemed like a complete fantasy, not to mention a complete headache when it came time to move; therefore, it was never a part of my college or Silicon Valley life. When the time came for my husband and me to look for our first house after we moved back to Ohio, I was magnetically attracted to the homes that either already had a piano or had a very clear place for a piano.

The day came when we found "the one" - the house that checked all of the boxes. Low traffic street: check. Pond with a fountain out back: check. Enough space for our puppy to roam: check. Room enough to grow a family: check. Piano in the living room: check. You're thinking: awesome, it all worked out. You got your piano. Wrong. Being novice negotiators, we didn't even think to ask to keep the piano. We later learned in a complete SMH (smack my head) moment that the previous owners would have been happy to leave it. The knowledge that we could have had this coveted item had me on high alert from that moment forward.

I must have put this out into the world enough that, one day, my manager at work said to me, "Weren't you looking for a piano?" "Why, yes I was," I replied. She told me that another one of our colleagues was trying to get rid of his piano. As long as we took care of moving it from his home, it was ours for the taking. After coordinating the great cross-city piano move of 2012, our living room was complete. I could have just as easily purchased an inexpensive keyboard (it would have been a similar cost and much less effort than the cross-city piano move) or tested out free piano apps on my phone, but there was something about the heft of the piano and the feel of the solid keys beneath my fingers that made this the right choice for me.

Now, eight years later, my occasional living room concerts help bring Her back, one 90s ballad or Broadway show tune at a time; but I am happiest when my daughter and husband do their daily practice, as they work toward their goal of learning the instrument.

The barrier here was access to the right equipment to do the thing that brought me joy. Oftentimes, we tell ourselves that it's going to be too much of a hassle, cost too much money, or take too much effort to procure the right materials and equipment. For people who dream of expressing themselves through art, it doesn't take an art studio with thousands of dollars of equipment. It might take a single trip to the art supply store. If you want to take up a sport that requires a lot of equipment, there might be a friend or neighbor looking to offload what is gathering dust in their basement - simply ask my friend, Ann, who borrowed my golf clubs for nine months; I was happy my neglected equipment was helping someone else remove a barrier to Her. If materials or equipment are the barrier for you, what plan can you create to gather the equipment at a low cost and minimal effort?

A few years past the acquisition of the piano, I had a chance to tackle the second barrier I built to music. I had a powerful conversation with my friend John, a leadership coach. He asked me what I valued to my core. What made me feel whole? Without hesitation, I said: music. The result was a realization that I wanted to make a concerted effort to bring music back into my life, other than the occasional living room concert or singing along to the radio on my daily commute. I walked away from that conversation with a simple action item. I said, "I'm going to join the choir." I attend church regularly and always like going to the 10:45 a.m. service because that is when the contemporary choir sings. I emailed the choir director soon after my conversation with John, and less than 24 hours later I was at my first choir practice. I was welcomed with open arms and given perhaps the greatest gift I could have asked for, a stack of sheet music I can use for living room concerts.

What was the barrier for me? I told myself it was time. My inner dialogue posed the question: "How can I possibly give up one night of the week for choir practice while raising two little kids and working these big jobs?" The natural follow-up coaching question was: "How true is it that I can't give up one night a week, and in reality, one hour a week in order to bring a little bit of Her back into my life?"

It wasn't true at all. I was already going to church every week and my husband was more than willing and capable of handling dinner clean-up and bedtime routine so I could do something I loved for ONE HOUR a week.

Let's be honest with ourselves - life stages happen. Things that, at one time, are a focal point become blurry. Yet, even though our situations in life change, the things we value and get our greatest joy from tend to be unwavering. There is something powerful about going back to the things that give you the greatest joy and sense of fulfillment. For me, it is my piano, sheet music, and singing in the choir.

*There is something powerful about going back to
the things that give you the greatest joy and sense
of fulfillment.*

The external barriers I had to remove were lack of materials and time, along
with the self-imposed family responsibilities. As I uncovered in the remembering and reconnecting sections how important music was to me, it became clear
that breaking through the barrier to the Her that came alive through music
required only a cast-off piano and once-a-week choir rehearsal.

Reflection Questions:
Recognizing and Removing External Barriers

- What external barriers are holding you back from Her?

- What action can you take to remove or minimize these barriers to bring something you used to love doing back into your life?

CHAPTER 12

Where External and Internal Barriers Meet

There is an interesting intersection where external and internal barriers meet. It's when external factors like time, resources, and obligations blend with a mindset that allows us to see only one way toward a solution. Breaking through this barrier requires us to shift our mindset. This shift hit me square in the face one day a few years ago and I haven't looked back.

One morning, I walked into my manager's office and said, "I've had an epiphany." I told her that I was looking at my Facebook feed and that morning there must have been a higher than usual number of "before and after" photos posted by friends who are health coaches and skin care consultants. My AH-HA thought was, "There is no before and after, there is no beginning and end." In order to sustain a healthy body weight or clear skin, what is required is a long term commitment to eating right, exercise, and hygiene regimens. There are no get-rich-quick or get-thin-quick programs that create sustainable change.

At that same time, I heard author Simon Sinek describe the difference between finite and infinite games.

Finite game = There is a set number of players, established rules, and clear determination of who wins or loses. There is a clear ending to the game. Most sports would fit into this category

Infinite game = Players change, rules change, desired outcomes change over time. This is ongoing. Most aspects of business and life are infinite games.

Sinek made the point that too many people focus on the finite game in business and in life. We are so focused on quarterly earnings and beating the competition that we don't think about the long game. In most cases, our focus on winning is misplaced, because everyone has a different definition of success and is chasing a different outcome. Add that misplaced focus to our need for instant gratification and we are faced with continual problems and lack of progress. The only way to create and sustain change is to focus on the long game.

Here is how this ties into my epiphany and the recognition and removal of barriers to Her. Like most busy working parents, I dislike chores and mundane tasks that always need to be done. I've read all of the blogs and Pinterest boards about "a clean house in 15 minutes a day" or "feed your family for a month on four hours of work." Those strategies haven't worked for me. It's because I was looking at the chores incorrectly. I was thinking of them as finite activities, when indeed they are infinite.

Here are things I wish were finite, but are indeed infinite:

- Laundry
- Dishes
- Cooking
- Cleaning
- Exercise
- Email

In that moment of realizing there is no before and after, I adjusted my attitude and approach to the daily grind. I have strategies to get through the chores or face the fact that there will always be dishes to do or laundry to fold. I put on a podcast or a great audiobook and get to work. On good days, I get my kids and husband to do the dishes and fold laundry.

Daily chores are one thing. When putting this into broader perspective, it's also important to shift our mindset and recognize that the following activities should always be treated as infinite:

- Relationships
- Health
- Education

- Personal Development
- Politics / public policy
- Religion and spirituality
- Care for the environment

What else would you classify as infinite to get closer to Her?

Because of this epiphany, I am a firm believer that NOW is always the best time to change our mindset or adopt new behaviors. I don't believe anything magical happens on December 31, so we don't have to wait until January 1 to begin an exercise program or eat more vegetables. On the flip side, we don't have to rush to complete things that aren't urgent and important before we ring in the new year.

This mindset shift to play the long game has been crucial to removing the barriers to Let Her Out. I've taken my share of before and after photos and crossed enough finish lines to know that life after a marathon or fitness challenge doesn't mean all-you-can-eat trips to the buffet in perpetuity. Finishing a book doesn't mean that I won't read another one. Completing a project at work doesn't mean that I'm on vacation for the rest of the year.

I've taken my share of before and after photos and crossed enough finish lines to know that life after a marathon or fitness challenge doesn't mean all-you-can-eat trips to the buffet in perpetuity.

As a recovering perfectionist and frequent box-checker, the realization that there is no beginning and there is no end has helped me ease up on these traits. They will always be part of me, so I will keep my red pen close by, but perhaps there will be less marks to make and boxes to check. Instead of focusing on the checkmarks, I look to the horizon to see what changes I can make today that will last into the future.

Reflection Questions:
Moving from Finite to Infinite

- How are you caught in the rat race of a finite game?

- How is that holding Her back instead of letting Her out?

- What mindset shifts can you make to push through this barrier?

CHAPTER 13

Removing Internal Barriers

Internal barriers likely started showing up for you before you even realized it. Reading my diary pages became an exercise of "spot the barrier." As early as the age of fifteen, I could see the barriers that started putting Her in the corner rather than in center stage. These emerged as deep-seated beliefs, limiting thoughts, and closely held emotions. For you, these scripts have been written from the time you were a young girl to the day you are reading this page. It's time to re-write the script so we can Let Her Out. The best way for me to help you spot the barriers you've erected is to show you mine.

What follows is a list of nine barriers that have been standing tall in my life for a long time. Some have come down and others are works in progress. As you work through these barriers, keep your pen nearby to take notes about what similarities and differences you face with your own barriers. Some may be evident to you before you even start this chapter, while others are buried so deep you will need time to reflect after finishing this section. After each section, I invite you to Pause & Reflect. For those barriers that resonate with you, spend time on the reflection. For those you don't connect to, keep moving. In order to support this work, you can download the Barrier Buster guide at letherout. com/resources to walk you through this section of the book.

Barrier: Lack of Recognition

Even though I've recounted my success on the high school stage, it was a journey to get to the starring role. Based on passages like the following, it's a wonder that I continued at all.

March 12, 1995 (age 15) - [About high school musical] I guess I'm just bummed because I haven't been noticed. I do everything right, maybe not outstanding, but I put forth 100% and get back nothing. I guess when you are just a "chorus person" you aren't noticed. Important yes, but noticed no. I guess that's just school politics for you. If you don't have a name you're nothing. If you aren't in the 'elite' group, you're nothing....I just hope some-day someone notices me for who I am...that day will come. When, I don't know, but I have faith that it will come.

August 10, 1995 (age 15) - Things change as you get older, more rec-ognized, and when you accomplish something great. I've never felt accepted as class president or anything else. I guess it takes a stronger person to take a step out of the crowd and try to get something done....if only people would recognize me and work with me, things would be great!

The barrier for me at the age of 15 became a barrier of recognition. I learned from a young age to give nothing or give it my all, and expected something in return for the effort. This lack of recognition and acknowledgement of my work caused me to back further into a corner versus try to stand out in center stage.

For some of you reading this, the idea of needing recognition isn't import-ant. For those of you who are cringing at the memory of giving it your all to receive nothing in return, the questions I pose to you are:

- Are you still waiting to be noticed?
- Are you waiting patiently for your turn for the promotion?
- Are you waiting for someone to ask you how you would run the organization?

Discomfort with and contempt for being in the shadows continued to fol-low me into my professional life. I have always given every role and organiza-tion I've been a part of 100% of me. Sometimes, that has been at the expense of showing up 100% for my family and friends. Sometimes, it's been at the ex-pense of sleeping from 2:30-4:30 a.m.; instead, replaying and rehearsing what I could do differently to be recognized.

How did I remove this barrier? I'd like to tell you that it faded away gradually and, by the time I was 30, I was cured of my need for recognition. Instead, what happened over a period of time was that I erected the barrier so high that the wrong social media post or picture on Instagram would send me into a blind rage or fit of tears.

As part of my corporate career, I led the 4,000-member women's resource group at the company. I lost more sleep and spent more discretionary time on this leadership role than any I'd ever held before, because real things were at stake; better parental leave policies, more women in executive roles, and pay equality are enough to get even the most conservative feminist riled up. I led meetings, organized steering committees, and had more after-hours chats with colleagues during my two-year term than I did in my day job. When the day came to pass the torch to the next president and executive board, I expected a little something for my efforts; perhaps, an inter-office thank you note, framed picture of the leadership team or even a bouquet of flowers I had heard so much about being the "prize" that women in senior leadership roles sent to those rising in the ranks. While I waited patiently at my desk for this token of appreciation, I sent personal thank you notes and matching bracelets to all of the volunteer board members who served with me. Still nothing came in my virtual or actual mailbox.

A few months after my term ended, the company won a pinnacle award in the realm of equality and women's leadership. I was beyond proud. I knew I had a part in that. Then, one night before bed, I opened my social media feed and saw a very large group of women and men from the company dressed up for the awards ceremony in New York City. As I was standing in my home office in my flannel pajamas and tattered slippers, I felt like I had been punched in the gut. I wasn't even invited to the party to celebrate the award I likely lost more sleep over than any other person at the company. I was red-behind-the-eyes mad. I went to bed with a stomach so tight it's a wonder I slept at all. I was fortunate to have a few good friends at work with whom I was able to share my full-sized frustration. Clearly the barrier had only grown.

Two years later, the women's group decided to award a member with the inaugural Inspiration Award. It was to go to a person who, through words, actions and attitude, inspired those who work with and around them. I knew I was deserving, but I had also learned by this point to keep my expectations low. One day, well in advance of the award announcement, I received a hand-written envelope in the mail. It was a simple nomination from a dear friend submitted on my behalf, proclaiming, *"Natalie has inspired me to think differently about what it means to be a woman in the workplace. She showed me what courage looks like to try new things, stand up for your beliefs and challenge social norms."* Standing in my foyer reading her words was the moment the barrier started coming down. I realized that the fancy party and formal gown wasn't what my life was about. It was about showing my peers that they can do more and be more than they ever thought. It was about showing them that they could be the change they wished to see in the world. The day I realized that recognition was more about how I show up and who I am authentic with than a trophy or photo opp was the day the barrier started to fade away. I ended up winning the award, but by that point, it was an honor, not a necessity, for me to keep inspiring those around me.

- How much of this story rings true for you? What is your equivalent of standing in your flannel jammies and slippers in a fit of red-behind-the-eyes rage?
- Are you still waiting for a tap on the shoulder, invitation to the party, or a moment to be discovered?

If you are waiting for recognition, I have one simple word that could save you the months of heartache and hundreds of moments of rage I have experienced on my journey: STOP. What is it that you really want? What I wanted was to know that what I did and how I spent my time made a difference. The only proof I had at the time that my leadership of the women's group mattered was the fancy awards ceremony. Once I could see another reality, that in truth, I was more of an inspiration to hundreds of women working their way up and around the ladder through the everyday interactions I had with them, I realized that I could stop pacing by the mailbox and, instead, keep making a difference.

The other antidote to my barrier of recognition has been to shower it fully on other people. This experience had me stock-up on thank you notes and time on my calendar that I spend saying "thank you" through a simple note, message or text. If you have a chance to make someone's day with your words of encouragement, don't think twice. Act. It may be what helps someone come out from the red-behind-the-eyes rage.

Pause & Reflect: Recognition

- How important is recognition to you?

- What is this barrier costing you in your personal and professional life?

Barrier: Feelings of Emptiness

The next barrier hit me like a ton of bricks as I was re-reading diary entries from my teenage years.

February 15, 1996 (age 16) - I haven't written lately. Life's really strange right now. I have so many things going for me. I'm applying to the State Fair Band. I am applying to be a 4-H counselor. I'm going to church camp to be a counselor...I just got home from Dinnerfest [the biggest annual fundraiser for the music programs at my school.] I did three things tonight that I always wanted to do. I accompanied the choir, I performed in show choir, and I played in the high school band. When I was little I thought those 3 things would be so awesome. I know 2 things. 1) We're just normal people in those groups and 2) I can reach any goal I want. I knew I wanted to do those things. It took 2 tries, but I'm there and loving it. I just am doing so much, but sometimes I feel so empty...

May 27, 1997 (age 17) - Right now I'm not feeling sad, just a little empty. I was filled so full a couple of months ago with thoughts of the future, now I'm backing up a little to remember the past...I guess life is like a puzzle. You work so hard to put the pieces together, but just end up taking it apart.

As a teenager, feeling empty was a deep emotion. When I spotted this barrier, so many things made sense. Accomplishments, awards and accolades are nothing if accompanied by the feeling of emptiness. Many of us are walking around empty. We give so much away on the path toward achievement that we miss out on the moments that matter along the way.

As an adult, emptiness has shown up on those days when I go non-stop from dawn until dusk (well, let's be really honest and say from pitch black to pitch black) and I wonder, "What did I accomplish today?" It's standing in your kitchen trying to make dinner while simultaneously hearing about the school day and latest work drama, and all you want to do is say: "Slow down. Talk one at a time. I can't do this. It's too much." At those moments, it's almost like I am so full that all I can feel is empty. I'm so full of ideas and problems and tasks and the next damn thing on the to-do list that I want to burst. The feeling this conjures in my body is that of blowing up a balloon to its last possible point. You use all possible energy from your lungs to get the balloon blown up and then with the tiniest bit of pressure, or the moment it touches a nearby surface, it pops into a pile of limp latex. The balloon was so full that all it could do was resort to being empty.

At those moments, it's almost like I am so full that all I can feel is empty.

How do we remove this barrier of emptiness? For me, it's a constant re-evaluation of what and who I let into my life. In order to focus fully on my family in those making-dinner-in-the kitchen moments, I have to remove all other distractions. When I feel the restless itch to do "one more thing," I make myself stop. I ask myself if that is the most important thing to be doing at that moment, if it can wait until later, or if it even needs to be done at all. What was once an over-planned and fully-stocked life has to be carefully curated in order to let just the right amount of things in, because when we fill it full of things and ideas and emotions, is when the balloon pops and we are left with emptiness.

How do you manage to stay sane amidst the demands, little hands, and crying voices that call for you at once? Do you resort to feeling empty? Do you numb it out with social media, wine or gossip? Do you nod your head in agreement when you are either not processing anything at all or screaming "No!" on the inside?

Along with removing distractions and being very careful of what and who gets let into my life, I've also learned that, in order to truly remove this barrier, you have to allow yourself to feel all of the feelings. This is how I described it in a blog post titled, "I was ALIVE Yesterday":

I was alive yesterday. And by alive, I don't mean "on fire" or "running on all cylinders."

I was sad. I was disappointed. I was proud. I was humbled. I was frustrated.

I was alive because I let myself feel these feelings. And I provided space for others to share theirs, too.

I led a session on vulnerability, courage and bravery for the women's group at my company. I shared my story of loss and a bit of my story of guilt. I heard others share their #metoo story, their admissions that they haven't been showing up fully at work and in life, that they play it safe, and stay quiet. In that room I saw so much potential. So much promise. Giving others space to turn these admissions into action plans reminded me of the power of speaking our truth. We have to strip down to our most vulnerable and truthful place to know where we really want to go in life. I joked that we would need Kleenex during the session. I was surprised that it was really true.

This experience was coupled with receiving both disappointing and shocking news throughout the day. I drove on the freeway and walked the aisles of stores trying to process these feelings. All of this "aliveness."

It was also during this time that I realized I was letting myself go numb. Who wouldn't want to feel numb when they are sad, disappointed, and frustrated?

Then I reminded myself that it's only through letting ourselves feel the tough feelings that we can experience the truly joyful feelings. If we are willing to FEEL, perhaps there wouldn't be so much pain in the world.

You have a choice: to be empty or to be alive. Are you going to try to tough it out or numb it out? Are you ready to embrace the low as much as the high? You have a choice about what you do with the balloon. You can fill it with just the right amount of air and create hours of volley-balloon fun, helium to delight, or water to create excitement. You don't have to fill your balloon to bursting.

Pause & Reflect: Emptiness

- How prevalent is the feeling of emptiness in your life?

- What is the effect on you and your relationships?

- What is one step you can take to begin breaking down this barrier?

Barrier: Dimming Ambition

Dimming ambition happens over decades. That's why you don't really see the day coming in your 30s, 40s or 50s when you wake up and ask yourself, "What happened to Her?" I used to have dreams of being in a place of power and politics. As far back as elementary school, I wanted to be the President of the United States of America when I grew up. Being raised in a small town made it easy to be involved in local politics. As mentioned earlier, I helped with my first school levy when I was in 8th grade and continued to cover local government as a newspaper reporter in high school. I visited Washington DC twice in high school for awards trips. I even ran for Lieutenant Governor at Buckeye Girls State, a week-long program designed to educate young women in the duties, privileges, rights, and responsibilities of good citizenship. Here's what these dreams and ambitions sounded like:

June 19, 1997 (age 17) - I don't think anyone ever stops learning or growing. I feel as if my world has gotten a bit smaller. This week also made me think about my future. My future could be in the Capitol Building, even the White House. It may be serving my country in ways I've never dreamed. I will be in Washington someday. Maybe walking on Pennsylvania Ave to see the 1600 block - and maybe to drive through the gates!

June 27, 1997 (age 17) Buckeye Girls State - This week has been full of extreme highs and low bottoms. I was on cloud nine as I was endorsed by my party and when I led 1,000 people in the Pledge of Allegiance. [I was one of the final candidates running for Lieutenant Governor.] I may not have gotten into the governor's office, but I have gotten into the hearts of everyone in my city. I wish everyday could be a bonding day with people, but I think it is our natural instinct to let people know how we feel about them at the latest point possible. I know one thing. Our Nation is great - and pretty soon - girls like me are going to be running it!

It's no wonder that I started college as a political science and journalism major, with intentions of going to law school and into politics. But what happened on my path to the Statehouse, Governor's Mansion and 1600 Pennsylvania Avenue? What dimmed this extremely big vision and level of ambition? This is what I uncovered when I dissected things that happened along the path that erected the barriers to Her desire to step into a position of power and politics.

Working at the House of Representatives - As a freshman in college, I worked as a Congressional Page at the Ohio Statehouse. Mostly, I fetched coffee, and occasionally a bagel for an elected official. An exciting day meant that I might get to make copies. Attending general sessions was about as dull as watching paint dry. I didn't get to talk to constituents about how laws affect them. I decided after six months that it would be more fun to work in a fast-paced campus job and I exchanged my uniform of khaki pants, white button-down shirt, navy blue blazer and ridiculous ladies bow tie for Ohio State sweatshirts and polos.

Living and working in Washington DC - My junior year in college, I participated in an internship program in Washington DC. Instead of working on Capitol Hill or at a think tank, I trekked to Silver Spring, Maryland every day to work for a healthcare non-profit. The work being done was extraordinarily meaningful and my internship project was a good lesson in getting legislation passed. What I couldn't understand at the time was: why did it take so many people and so much money to pass a bill that was a no-brainer? We were working to have a less-invasive, lower-cost chemotherapy treatment covered by health plans. No one on either side of the aisle was opposed to this happening, yet it took thousands of dollars, hundreds of hours, and countless trips back and forth from Maryland to the Hill to make it happen.

My two immersions into government didn't make me eager to go to law school. I kept the political science major, mostly because I had nearly all of the credits completed, and added a second major in psychology because it interested me more. By this time, Rob was in graduate school at Stanford and, soon after I left Washington DC, we got engaged. In rapid succession after I graduated from Ohio State, we got married and I moved across the country. California seemed like the farthest I could get from Pennsylvania Avenue, both geographically and ideologically. Unlike the barrier of recognition, which grew steadily over time, the barrier of dimming my ambition seemed to happen on that one-way flight to California. Not for a minute do I regret these choices, but one day in my late 30s it hit me and I asked myself: what happened to the girl who wanted to be President? What could have changed my course? What could have kept me on a path to 1600 Pennsylvania Avenue? Here is the list I've come up with to inspire all of us to propel one another forward toward our dreams and ambitions, whether related to politics or not.

Mentor young women - When you see yourself in the promise and optimism of young women, step in to mentor them. We need to stay close as life happens to them.

Become engaged at all levels of community and government - Posting an anti-this or pro-that on social media won't accomplish much. We need to become educated, voice our opinion and TAKE ACTION on issues at the local, state, and national levels.

Bring focus to the impact of public policy on women and minorities - Women and minorities are negatively affected by numerous public policies and pending legislation. Think health care, minimum wage laws and parental leave. It's important to take a minute to walk in the shoes of those affected to put a face on our laws and fuel our activism.

Make a difference in YOUR own way - Perhaps politics and public policy are far from the place where you want to devote your time and energy. What other ways can you lift others up as you continue to rise on your own journey?

While I feel like I am doing my life's work, I'm also not done working through this barrier. My late 30s wake up call was that the country still needs my strong voice. I'm going to get my head out of the sand. It was easy to burrow as life happened. Whether it's an occasional call to my Senator or Representative, attending a local city hall meeting, or simply following the pending legislation to be fully informed, I can make a difference. A future run for office remains unseen, but I will never say never.

My key to becoming re-engaged is to remind myself that real people are affected by laws and policies. I will walk in their shoes and take action from there. The following is my mantra as I pivot from my childhood dreams and ambitions to a place where I can make a difference today:

Not a single person in this world chose where, how and to whom they were born. All of us have a great opportunity - or perhaps even an obligation - to understand our differences and embrace diversity.

I am proud of where I come from and the path I took to get where I've gotten, but that doesn't mean I can ignore the path of others. I'm writing this book at the height of what I will call the new civil rights era. We've got to understand, appreciate, and advocate for people who have a steeper hill to climb because of systemic racism and discrimination. That's where I'm going to focus my ambition when it comes to politics and public policy.

Dimming ambition came in the form of backing away from my dreams of politics. While I might not be showing up on a ballot anytime soon, what this barrier has shown me is that there can be another path to fuel the ambition and get to the desired outcome. While I might not be delivering campaign speeches and writing legislation, I am speaking and writing in order to make a difference in the lives of others. I hope this section will inspire you to declare your race or take back your ambition.

Pause & Reflect: Dimming Ambition

- Where have you dimmed your ambition?

- What did you want to be when you grew up? Does part of you still wonder what it would be like to do that thing?

- How can you redefine ambition in order to bring Her forward?

Barrier: Impostor Syndrome

The next barrier takes us right back to one of the opening stories of this book. I want to share how winning that 4-H purple ribbon has influenced all of the future purple ribbon moments in my life. When I first learned about the impostor syndrome, which materializes as continual doubt in accomplishments and fear of being exposed as a "fraud", I thought about the purple ribbon I won that day at the Ohio State Fair for my oatmeal cookie demonstration. The feelings I had that day were a combination of disbelief and excitement. Even at the age of 9, I clung to that well-deserved award with a feeling of "not enough-ness" that accompanies so many of life's great accomplishments. Who, me? Can't be. They must have it wrong.

The subsequent purple ribbon moments that followed in my life – being elected to leadership positions in college groups, hired for internships, asked to join non-profit boards in my early 20s - were always accompanied by similar feelings of disbelief and excitement. In many of those instances, I didn't want to check the election results or answer the call when the hiring manager's number was on caller ID. I wouldn't win or be the one selected. Someone would catch on that I didn't know what I was doing. Certainly, there would be more qualified people to select.

This impostor syndrome was both dormant and ever-present as I started my post-college life. When Labor Day comes around each year, I am reminded of my one-way flight to California in 2002. I was a newlywed with no job, no apartment, no car and no local friends. I had my new husband, a new degree from The Ohio State University, and a bucket of emotions – hope, fear, excitement, nervousness. What I also had was my small town spirit – a spirit that led me to seek out community, mobilize my network, and get to know people. That's how this small town girl made Silicon Valley feel like home for four years.

2002 was a tough job market in the Bay Area. I knew I wanted to work in the nonprofit or higher education sector and had been diligently looking for roles in those fields for the previous six months. Little panned out and I knew I'd be spending my first several weeks applying and interviewing for jobs. One of our first stops after we landed from that cross-country flight was to my husband's lab on the Stanford University campus. I checked my email for the first time in seven days. I had received a message seven days prior, letting me know about the informational interview I was invited to at Stanford. I missed the window during my wedding and honeymoon. I was not deterred and replied that I was on my honeymoon, missed his email, and hoped he could meet me that week. I ended up getting that job and, to this day, have the greatest respect and admiration for my former colleagues and friends at the Stanford Alumni Association.

After four years as an over-programmed college student, I took full advantage of my only obligation being a nine-to-five gig during my first few months in California. I took step aerobics classes, read for leisure, and watched TV. A lot of TV. It was during one of my marathon show-nights that I realized I had to stop this bad habit. That led to some amazing opportunities getting to know people in my community. It included stops at the Palo Alto YMCA, where I served as both a board member and a personal trainer. I joined, and eventually led, the Bay Area Buckeyes OSU alumni club. And the crown jewel of my time in California – completing a triathlon through the Leukemia and Lymphoma Society Team in Training program (more on that later). I met amazing people during this time. Some like me – small town implants only there for a few years, some native Bay Area residents who were thankful they bought into the housing market earlier in life, and many people from other countries who were able to call the Bay Area and United States their new home.

A lot happened in Silicon Valley when I lived there. Facebook was born. Google went public. Apple invented the iPod. I didn't appreciate that this was happening around me. It wasn't until I read the biography of Steve Jobs and watched *The Social Network* that I realized how close I lived to innovators and entrepreneurs who changed the world. I was just a 20-something girl from a small town, trying to get by in order to pay my $1,800/month rent.

All in all, this is a beautiful part of the story: Small town girl conquers Silicon Valley. What isn't shared in this version is that, every day, I was afraid. I was afraid someone would figure out that I didn't belong there. Behind closed doors, my husband and I talked about how we would have done very well at Stanford as undergrads, but neither of us would have been accepted. Every day when I stepped into my student advising role, I wondered why these students were coming to me, a small town girl from Ohio, when they were the ones living the dream. This impostor syndrome led me to avoid those who were making it big in the tech scene. Surely, they had something I didn't. Surely, they knew a secret handshake that let them into their world full of stock options and IPO promises. While I wouldn't trade my California experience for anything, I often wonder how it could have been different if I hadn't been so afraid. I would have had different conversations, asked more powerful questions, and perhaps put myself on the line for bigger opportunities, instead of staying small and comfortable in the job I was very good at, but that didn't stretch me.

While I wouldn't trade my California experience for anything, I often wonder how it could have been different if I hadn't been so afraid.

Somewhere in the "ah-has" of my late 30s, after a series of promotions, elected leadership roles, and invitations to speak, advise and coach, I understood that I'm not an impostor. I earned those ribbons. I was a success in Silicon Valley. My only regret is living so much of that part of my life in fear.

All too often, we convince ourselves we've lost before we even give ourselves a chance. We must remind ourselves that we are worthy of the space we occupy. Don't question your success. Wear your ribbons proudly. Own your achievements and use them to shape your future plans.

Pause & Reflect: Impostor Syndrome

- How often are you living in fear versus stepping into opportunity?

- How often do you find yourself doubting your recognition or achievements? How can you connect to Her in order to remind yourself that you are worthy and earned the award or the recognition?

- What would your life look like if you removed the barrier of impostor syndrome and instead you stepped into the shoes of confidence? What if you enjoyed your success and accomplishments?

Barrier: Disconnection and Loneliness

One of the saddest moments I had as an adult was when I realized that I had developed a barrier of disconnection that led to extreme loneliness. You would never have known this from looking at me, the small town girl who regularly gave seminars on networking and styled myself as a relationship management expert. Because I grew up in such a small town, I was used to everyone knowing everything about everyone else. For some of my fellow small town alumni, this was the worst part about small town life. For me, it was one of my favorite parts of growing up in a small town. Because I already knew where people lived and where their parents worked and what sport they played, I could bypass small talk and get beneath the surface, fast. I was born and raised ready to go a level deeper with people.

As I ventured out into the big world, other people weren't always so ready to get real and deep, fast. As a young adult, I shared my passionate views with groups of friends. They looked at me like I was crazy, wondering why I had to have an opinion at all. In the corporate world, I dared to be bold with my viewpoints, only to receive stern looks from senior leaders that suggested, "You're entering dangerous territory." And somewhere along the way, life became more about likes, comments and shares on social media than it did about actual connection.

This is when the barrier of disconnection and loneliness was built. If people weren't willing to go all in with me, then they wouldn't get the front row seat to the real me, either. This was the wake-up call I had in the middle of 2018. I decided to write a year-long blog series called 52 Weeks of Meaningful Connections. (It's still available for bingeing or through a free weekly email subscription at smalltownleadership.com/52weeks.) Part way through writing this series, which covered everything from writing introduction emails to talking to strangers, and getting to know co-workers in meaningful ways, I woke up and realized that I was so damn lonely.

I was lonely because no one really knew me anymore. I had formed an opinion that most people didn't want to connect below the surface, so I stayed on the surface, made artificial small talk, or no talk at all. Because of this pulling back, not only did I build a barrier around myself, but I built a barrier around people who I really wanted to have relationships with.

In order to tear down this barrier, I shifted what I wrote in the year-long blog series. Instead of giving tactical advice on a proper LinkedIn invitation (for the love of all that is good, please include a personalized message - ALWAYS!), I wrote posts about suffering when we don't share (Week 35), judgement and connection (Week 46); and authenticity (Week 49).

Week 52 wasn't a confetti-filled cake celebrating a year of meaningful connections. It was an emotionally charged piece titled *So Damn Lonely*. In it, I challenged readers to get past small talk and get to know one another, even if they don't agree, think they have nothing in common, and most importantly, even if it gets uncomfortable.

Admitting to being lonely was the step I needed to take to face the barrier of disconnection. The epilogue to the series was the moment the barrier to disconnection and loneliness dissolved. Here's what I had to say:

Connection starts from the inside and works its way out.

You have to be connected to you.

Why have I felt so damn lonely? I was lonely for a lot of reasons. I experienced:

- *Loneliness in perfection*
- *Loneliness in productivity*
- *Loneliness in parenting*
- *Loneliness in fear*
- *Loneliness in the unknown*
- *Loneliness in being "put together"*
- *Loneliness in busyness*
- *Loneliness in leadership*
- *Loneliness in lacking recognition*
- *Loneliness in nodding my head 'Yes', when inside I was screaming "NO"*

Mainly, I was lonely because I wasn't connected to myself. When you can't be yourself, you can't be with others in a meaningful way. It's isolating when you aren't being YOU – no matter the reason. That is the ultimate barrier to connection. There is a path forward, though. (Important Distinction: A path. A journey. Not a silver bullet.)

Much like business leaders are getting better at identifying the why and purpose of their organizations, you need to get clear on:

- *Who you are*
- *How you want to show up*
- *Who people get to see in the world*

Then you will be a magnet for meaningful connections. You will be more connected to your family. Your community. Your work. All starting with you. It took me 52 weeks to sort through all of this. For you, it might be the same. For the next 52 Weeks, I have vowed to bring my full self and

my core values to each interaction I have: family, leadership, ambition &
connection.

How will you bring your full self forward? What values are you bring-
ing with you in your next 52 weeks? What could your life look like a year
from now if you stepped into those values fully?

I was done being so damn lonely and I invite you to join me on my continual quest for deeper connection.

Pause & Reflect: Loneliness & Disconnection

- How much do you resonate with the sentiment of being "So
  Damn Lonely?"

- What is on your loneliness list that has built up walls to other
  people and meaningful relationships?

- Who can help you feel less lonely and disconnected?

Barrier: My Body

Back in the remembering, I told you about my 15-0 perfect serve volleyball
game, the 4x100 track championship, and overcoming being cut from the volleyball team by creating my own fitness routine and home gym. I left out an
important part of this story. It's one of the biggest barriers that has kept me
from fully loving and appreciating my body and my strength. The moment
when things changed was when I was nine years old. I wrote this in my diary.
"She said I was fat. So what. I don't really care any way. It's not how a person looks.
It's how they act and my ippion [opinion] I'm nice!" Until that moment in time, I
was beautiful and strong. I wouldn't hesitate to skinny dip or wear a crop top
or dance on a stage with strangers. I was one with my body. At age nine, this

relationship with my body and my strength became distorted. Through the remembering and reconnecting, I have looked at enough photos and re-lived enough memories where I simply want to put my arms around that young girl and say, "You are beautiful. You are strong. Do not let those three words 'You are fat'" mess with your head."

Mess with my head is exactly what they did. Throughout my childhood and young adulthood, I exercised and played sports for equal parts recreation and body image maintenance. I never wore a two-piece bathing suit. I always covered up my midriff. I learned about calories in and calories out in high school and packed myself countless school lunches of plain turkey sandwiches and baby carrots. I want to be clear: I never entered eating or exercise disorder territory. My mom is the best cook and baker in Seneca County and there are certain things I would never miss out on in this life, mainly anything my mom cooks or bakes. What didn't manifest as a disorder manifested as distortion, and sometimes obsession.

There were several times on the journey when I was 100% happy with my appearance and body. Even then, my mind would not let up and I had to keep digging deeper, getting stronger, and eat yet another turkey sandwich. This barrier to my own strength kept me playing small a lot in my life. I would no longer take the stage in the same way. I would take it only if I could manage the narrative and if I could crop out the photos. The whole time, my facade of confidence would hide the low self-esteem I was truly feeling on the inside.

This barrier to our body, strength, and true self causes many women to hide. We hide our body. We hide our dance moves. We wear things that provide cover and serve as protective armor from the words that can hurt so bad: You are fat. This is a barrier that becomes shellacked to us and takes years to peel away.

Removing this barrier continues to be a work in progress. If you are a teenager or twentysomething reading this book, my advice to you is: be strong, love your body and challenge your mind and body equally as you become who you are meant to be. To the women in their 30s, 40s and 50s, my advice is exactly the same.

I learned to love my body only by challenging it; sometimes purposefully, sometimes by accident. My years of basement step aerobics, which I continued at Ohio State, gave me tendonitis. I could have given it up, but I loved the art and order of a step-lined gym thundering with the latest dance mix. I underwent physical therapy and added in water aerobics, yoga and weight lifting. When I got married at the age of 22, I thought I was in the best shape of my life. I weighed 107 pounds, had an artificial tan, whitened teeth and still ate a lot of turkey sandwiches. I know I looked beautiful on that day and, looking back, I know I would have been equally as beautiful at 125 pounds, natural tan, and less white teeth.

Moving across the country after getting married meant that I had to find a place to continue my step aerobics habit and I found that quickly through Stanford Aerobics. Without fail, I was always first in line to get my front row spot. All of the aerobics, combined with using a bike as my main mode of transport, meant that I stayed in fairly decent shape as a newlywed. This was also the early 2000s when fad diets seemed to be even more popular than ever. I tried the Adkins diet, but soon realized a full breakfast of eggs and bacon every day was not good for my genetically high cholesterol.

It was about this time in my mid-twenties that my sister took a job with the Leukemia and Lymphoma Society's Team In Training program, where she helped people train for endurance athletic events while they fundraised for the organization. Even though she worked for the Cleveland office, every year they brought a team to participate in the Wildflower Triathlon at Lake San Antonio, California, about three hours from the San Francisco Bay Area. She flew in for the race one year and said, "You really should do this."

Throughout college and my early 20s, I claimed that I was not a runner. If you know anything about triathlons, it's that there are equal parts swimming, biking and running. Swimming I had down. As part of living the California life, I decided to re-take swim lessons as an adult and swam in the beautiful Olympic-caliber aquatics center at Stanford on many lunch breaks. The year-around tan this brought was an awesome side benefit to the anaerobic capacity I built. I also biked to and from work and all around campus, so I was ready for biking. But running. Ugh. (Oreos, Ricki Lake - need I say more?)

Finally, our last year to be in California rolled around and I decided I better get working on this sister-prescribed bucket-list item. I signed up to attend the kick-off meeting for the 2006 Wildflower Triathlon, where they outlined the equipment you needed, along with the amount of money you were required to raise. Both were substantial. Rob attended the meeting with me. I was getting ready to fill out the paperwork when he looked at me and said, "I think I want to do it, too." I was caught completely caught off guard because he was in the midst of finishing his postdoctoral work at Stanford and was at the lab all hours, day and night. I said, "Ok, are you sure?" He was, and at the ages of 26 and 28, we signed up for our first triathlon.

We made time for the six-days-a-week training schedule. On Monday and Wednesday, we met at the pool and swam during lunch time, and in the evenings we ran on the treadmill or headed out for short runs. On Tuesday, we biked. On Thursday, the team gathered for a group bike ride or track workout. We did both on the same night the closer we got to race day. Friday was our day off and we were usually asleep on the couch by 8pm. Saturday was the long team practice, which was typically a swim followed by a long bike ride. On Sunday, we met up casually with other members of the team for trail runs.

To say this event changed our lives, and my perspective on my body and strength, would be an understatement. What you have to understand about doing a triathlon in California is that it is NO JOKE. The swim was in a frigid lake, so we learned to rely on a wetsuit for both warmth and buoyancy. The bike began with a one-mile uphill stretch. You may think I'm exaggerating, but I'm not. I was determined NOT to be the person who simply walked her bike up the hill, so I learned the art of climbing hills on a bike. (Pro tip: low gear, fast spins.) Then I was met with a hilly 10-K run. I was about to the point when I wanted to give up and walk to the finish, when I saw an 83-year old woman on the trail in front of me. (During these races, your age is written in sharpie on your body in three different places.) I thought, "Oh, hell no! She is not beating me!" and I made my way to the finish line.

Since crossing that finish line, I have lost count of the number of finish lines I have crossed for subsequent triathlons, 5Ks, half and full marathons. I continued training for endurance athletic events after moving back to Ohio and knew I wanted to complete a full marathon before starting our family. I crossed that finish line in 2008. The knowledge that my body was able to do those things has helped chip away at the barrier of my strength.

What ultimately helped me appreciate my body and my strength was carrying and delivering both of my daughters naturally. My first daughter came two weeks early and needed a bit of prodding to enter the world. I remember being moved to the postpartum room after 9 hours of labor and bursting into tears.

The nurse looked at me with deep concern. All I had for her in response was, "I'm so happy." Two and a half years later, my youngest daughter, Katie, decided she couldn't wait to enter the world and was born within two hours of my first contraction. There was no time for an epidural. I remember locking eyes with the nurse in the delivery room and saying, "I'm going to do whatever you tell me to do." Katie came into the world kicking and screaming and hasn't stopped since. Later that year, I wrote the following blog for the Columbus Marathon.

Things I've done in 2 hours or less: Completed the Columbus ½ Marathon & Delivered a Baby

In a guest blog from 2010 I told you my reason for running was "No More Fat Pants" after having my first baby. Two years and another baby later, I'm training again for the ½ marathon. I've completed a fair amount of endurance events in the past six years (six triathlons, 4 half marathons and one full marathon to be exact), but I had no idea how significant that training was until this March.

March 5 (week 39 of my pregnancy) was a normal day. I worked at home, made a few dinners for the freezer, cleaned up toys and was getting ready to settle in for a nap. Then my contractions started. Then they kept coming 2 minutes apart. After a lightning fast drive from Dublin to the Ohio State campus and bypassing the hospital admissions line, I was faced with the option of delivering the baby naturally in a few pushes or waiting it out for an epidural to kick in. In that moment I visualized all of the hills I have climbed and finish lines I have crossed and I knew I had one choice: go for it.

Barely 2 hours past my first contraction and 15 minutes after entering the delivery room, my second daughter was born. When they handed me my baby girl, the only thought going through my head was "I can't believe I just did this!" Once I recovered from the shock of going from zero to baby in 2 hours, I realized that my childbirth experience was much like an endurance event. You prepare for months, along the way working through aches and pains and sleepless nights, and in that single moment when you cross

*the finish line, it is all worth it. That day will forever serve as a reminder
to me of what can be accomplished in two hours.*

My goal is to make physically challenging experiences a normal part of my life. Most of them don't require naturally delivering a baby in two hours, but they include continued participation in 4-milers, 10Ks and half marathons. I'm always eager to try out a new class in my basement workout space or at the actual gym. I've even worked with personal trainers off and on so I could learn how to properly lift heavy weights. While I strive for a healthy diet, I don't eat nearly as many turkey sandwiches as I used to and I let myself indulge in all of the baked goods made by my mom. More than anything, I don't waste time focusing on what I could, should or need to look like. Removing the barrier to my strength and my body is a continual climb.

Pause & Reflect: Your Body

- How have your perception and feelings about your body turned into a barrier?

- What physical challenges have you faced or overcome to remind you of your strength?

- What action do you want to take to remind yourself of your strength and power?

Barrier: Hiding the Pain of Adulthood

A significant internal barrier many women face is hiding their pain. We do it for many "good" reasons. We don't want to make other people uncomfortable. We are ashamed. We are afraid. Once I recognized one of the most significant instances of hiding my own pain, I was able to shed light on it and share it for the benefit not only of myself, but for others, too.

My moment was a miscarriage in 2011. I was already visualizing the pregnancy announcement: *Baby #2 to make an arrival on 11/11/11! Joining big sister who was born on 10/10!* Then the moment came when something didn't seem right. I began experiencing signs that I understand now are indicative of a miscarriage. I called Rob. He asked if we should call the doctor. We agreed to wait and see if my symptoms continued. I went on with my day and attended a networking event that night, in a complete haze the entire time. The signs continued.

We called the doctor that night (a Friday) and she said there wasn't much we could do at that point. We could wait things out through the weekend and she would see me on Monday. When the signs continued throughout the weekend, we made the decision to go to the emergency room on Sunday morning. Patience isn't something we had at that moment.

During that ER visit, we learned that there was no heartbeat. My pregnancy was at eight weeks and the doctor estimated that the baby did not live past six weeks. We were able to let things unfold naturally and I miscarried the baby. It was a very tough time, both because we lost the baby, and also because we hadn't announced the pregnancy. At the time, we felt that there was no way to share what we were going through except with a close circle of friends and family.

The loss, combined with the hiding, was depressing and defeating. After I returned to work, the thought that stuck in my mind was: the baby lived for six weeks. I thought about my life during that six weeks. Was I doing meaningful work? Was I making a contribution? Was I happy at work? The answer to all of those questions was "No". That's when I looked at myself in the mirror and said: "You will make every day count." It's also when I printed out this quote from Steve Jobs' 2005 Stanford Commencement Speech (the year Rob graduated with his PhD) and taped it to my computer monitor at work where I would look at it every day.

"Your time is limited, so don't waste it living someone else's life. Don't be trapped by dogma — which is living with the results of other people's thinking. Don't let the noise of others' opinions drown out your own inner voice. And most important, have the courage to follow your heart and intuition. They somehow already know what you truly want to become. Everything else is secondary."

The first barrier I removed was for myself. I used this experience of loss to propel myself forward. I told myself that the baby I lost came into my life for a reason. The reason was to help me make every day count. From there, I started pursuing different work. I said "yes" to opportunities more often. I shared this story with people I trusted. I ended up getting pregnant a few months later and we had Katie eleven months after the miscarriage.

Even at the time of writing this, 9 years later, nothing has been the same since her birth. I changed roles at work (twice), took on the leadership of the women's group at my company, became a professional coach and started Small Town Leadership. Through all of this, I've remembered that my baby – the one who lived six weeks – gave me the greatest gift I've ever been given in my 30's. A gift to make every day count.

The second barrier that was finally removed came when I shared this story openly on my blog and through videos many years later. The message I shared with others was: you don't have to keep this a secret. You do not have to be ashamed. The private messages, posts, and phone calls of quiet crying that followed told me that removing this barrier of hiding pain is likely the hardest, yet most powerful barrier we can remove for ourselves and one another.

Somewhere, we have scripted in our head to keep everyone around us comfortable and safe. It causes us to look outside of ourselves every minute of every day. By the time we muster the energy to look inside ourselves, we tell ourselves that the effort to share our pain and heartache is simply not worth it.

Somewhere, we have scripted in our head to keep everyone around us comfortable and safe.

When you can start to share your story, even the lowest, deepest, saddest parts, you can start to see Her in a new light. She starts to feel like she can actually emerge from the shadows.

Pause & Reflect: Pain of Adulthood

- What is it costing you to keep everyone around you comfortable?

- What would it feel like to release some of your pain, if only to a few close friends?

- Who might benefit from hearing your story?

Barrier: Busyness of Early Parenthood

I often refer to the period of my life where things were a complete blur as "throes of early parenthood." Typically, this phrase helps other new parents feel like they don't have to have it all together. In 2008, soon after I graduated with my MBA and had started the first corporate job of my career, I decided I was going to launch my public speaking career. Now that I had this MBA and fancy job, the bright lights and big stages would be mine for the taking. As luck would have it, a professor from business school started a new website connecting speakers to event planners at the same time (for my fellow speakers reading wondering about this holy grail, it has since shuttered.) I quickly created a profile, and within days was the first person to book an (unpaid) speaking gig through this site. I didn't care that I had to drive two hours; this was my chance to prove that I was the next big thing on the speaking circuit. Soon after I confirmed this opportunity, I got pregnant with my first child. I was in week 9 of pregnancy when this speaking opportunity came around. I wasn't quite showing, but felt like I needed to run to the restroom every three minutes.

This speaking opportunity went off without a hitch. I came into the event, a fresh-faced 29-year old, and showed this group of veteran business owners that a small town girl can help you build your network more effectively. Much of the post-event feedback said, "I wasn't expecting to learn anything from a 20-something, but she delivered." After the event, when I was enjoying the obligatory chicken lunch with the event coordinators, one of them leaned over to me and said, "When are you due?" I looked at her big-eyed and said, "How did you know?" She told me she just did. I told her that the next day was when I was going to tell my parents that they were going to become grandparents, and she dare not tell. So here I was, between the biggest breakthrough of this speaking career, and the most important moment for my family.

I continued to seek out small speaking opportunities that came directly as a result of the first one, but as the summer wore on, my belly got bigger; it was harder to speak without losing my breath, and the clincher - when I arrived at a venue to deliver yet another free presentation on networking, clearly eight months pregnant, almost starting to lose my voice, and was told I couldn't bring in my water bottle, I about lost it. I paid the bartender $2 for a bottle of water, delivered as well as I could, and got in my car and said to myself, "I'm done. I've got other things to focus on."

And that is exactly what I did for the next seven years. I focused on my family. I focused on those babies. I focused on trying to get rest and heal and strengthen my body. I focused on my corporate career.

THE BREAKTHROUGH: And then, one day, I woke up and had another slap-in-the-face moment that said, "You can have big dreams AND little kids." And I began to remove the barrier. I hired a coach. I began putting myself back out there for speaking opportunities. I began writing. If you feel like parenthood is your barrier to Letting Her Out, these are the five things I've done to chase BIG DREAMS while raising LITTLE KIDS. It's a blueprint you can adapt to help you chase your dreams whether you have little kids, big kids or no kids.

1) **Hire a coach** – In order to get really clear on where you want to go on the most efficient path, hire someone to help you get on track. This is what I did in 2015. Not only did it lead to the idea for Small Town Leadership, but it sped my path to making it happen. If you are the type of person who appreciates tough questions and likes to be held accountable for progress, a coach can be your ticket to success. Coaching changed my life. It could be the best investment you make in yourself at this point in your life, too.

2) **Find and use your "Fringe Hours"** – I learned about the concept of fringe hours from author, Jessica N. Turner, when she was interviewed for a podcast back in 2015. The fringe hours are where the Pomodoro Technique (focusing solely on one thing for 25 minutes) meets those small pockets of

time when your kids are a) in bed b) watching a 22 minute cartoon or c) participating in their weekly dance/soccer/karate class or any other activity that doesn't require your full attention. This is your time to get things done. I've built, rebuilt, written, recorded, and created more content in these fringe hours than any other blocks of time. The fringe hours can be your time to make progress on you.

3) Write it down – If you have an idea, strike while the iron is hot and write it down! When I scramble for a piece of paper or my digital note-taking app, I continually remember Bruce, the motivational speaker who came to my high school, telling us that the reason 97% of people don't achieve their dreams is because they don't write them down. I want to be part of the 3% who make things happen and, after five years of diligent practice, I believe in his guidance more than ever. In addition to Post-its galore on my desk, I keep a running Google doc titled "Unpublished Content." When an idea hits, I write it down. If I have 10 minutes when the flash hits, I write as much as I can in the moment. (That's how most of this book came to be.)

In addition to capturing these in-the-moment thoughts, I also write down my accomplishments and goals on a monthly basis. I look back at the content I created and delivered, the coaching clients I served, the connections I nurtured, and the progress I made toward my larger goals. Then, I craft a set of goals for the upcoming month. This usually takes me 15 minutes, and sets the course for a productive month ahead.

4) Lean on your partner or close friends – I couldn't have done half of the things I've done in the past five years without Rob's support. I traveled a lot for my corporate jobs and travel equally as much as a professional speaker, consultant and coach. I also have regular commitments in the evenings and weekends. I used to have extreme guilt at leaving the family to chase these dreams, but now I realize that I'm a role model for my daughters. They are learning from me what it takes to be a leader and build a business. I'm also showing other young mothers that it's OK to put your partner in charge while you go after your dreams.

I knew that this was working the day my husband received his winter teaching schedule when our daughters were one and three. He was assigned to teach a class at 8:00 a.m. three days a week. He was the designated day care drop-off parent and couldn't fathom how he would get two babies wrangled into their winter gear and manage the commute to campus. He calmly responded to his boss and said, "My wife travels frequently for work and making it to campus by 8:00 a.m. with the winter commute is going to be tough, if not impossible." His boss quickly replied, "Oh, I didn't think of that. We will get you reassigned." This *Lean In* moment will always make me proud and hopeful for future generations of parents who are trying to figure out how to navigate shared responsibilities.

I'm fortunate to have Rob as my partner on this journey. If you are navigating without a partner, it is worth creating a support system of people who are not only cheering you on, but who are ready, willing and able to help with daycare pickup or the early morning shift so you can focus on your dream.

5) Identify the right time to get started – You will always be able to come up with a dozen reasons why now is not the right time to pursue your dreams. What if I challenge you on this and simply state that: *Now is the perfect time for you to pursue your dreams.* Waiting for your kids to be out of diapers will turn into waiting for your kids to start kindergarten, which will turn into waiting for your kids to graduate from high school. By then, your dream may be lost. You might lose yourself in the process. The next 10, 12, or 18 years are going to pass by quickly, whether or not you are pursuing your dreams. Why not jump in and make it happen, NOW? Your kids, partner, friends and family deserve to see you showing up for yourself as much as you show up for them.

If you already have your big idea, this should be a good blueprint to get you started. If you don't know where to even start with your big dream, hire a coach or use some of your fringe hours to explore. Enlist the support of your partner to help you get started. Don't let having little kids get in the way of your big dreams. You are showing them a way forward that will stick with them for a lifetime.

Pause & Reflect: Busyness of Early Parenthood

- How often are you using parenthood or your particular life stage as a barrier that prevents you from chasing your dreams?

- What is one step of the blueprint you can use to help you begin to remove the barrier?

Removing the Barrier to my own Power

A major "ah-ha" I had while writing this book is that my purpose statement is to *be real while being in power*. One of the significant internal barriers I've faced as a professional woman has been being real while being in power. By 'in power', I mean being in leadership roles, both formal and informal, inside and outside of organizations. I feel like I'm being real most of the time, but if I had to flip through the filmstrip of my life, I'm probably 50/50 on real versus covering or putting on a brave, fake, or otherwise false front. This is likely the reason I ask all of my coaching clients: "Who gets to see the real you?" I ask them this question because I see them fully. In the confines of confidentiality and trust, they let me see them. And they are beautiful. And intelligent. And powerful. And assertive. And insightful. And they don't see it. Which begs the question: who gets to see the real you?

The "ah-ha" for me came smack-dab in the middle of writing this book, during a marketing course I was taking. You see, I was trying everything I could to overcome the barriers that were keeping me safely in my corporate job and holding me back from my dreams. I took all of the classes, listened to all of the podcasts, and read all of the books. I wanted one of those resources, authors or teachers to have the answer. I wanted them to reassure me that I could comfortably replace my corporate salary when I became 100% self employed. I wanted them to give me the formula.

In the midst of the search for this answer, Bill, the teacher of the marketing class, asked us to think about someone we admired and to complete a series of statements about that person. Those statements, which were focused on a hero in my life, culminated in the following: "I am being real while being in power in order to show others a path to a better life." The joke was on me, as he let us know that this was our purpose statement. Of course we had the chance to wordsmith and edit, but ultimately, this was the core of why we do what we do.

Be real WHILE being in power. Whew. This is the barrier that so many of us are trying to break through. What does being real even mean? Does it mean showing up with our natural roots and makeup-free face? Does it mean letting the thoughts that only circle in our head come out of our mouth? Does it mean disclosing that we don't know all of the answers? Your realness is what the world needs from you. I recognize it's what those closest to me have benefited from for so long and I'm tired of keeping it to that inner circle.

Pause & Reflect: Power

- What does being real mean to you?

- Who gets to see you and know you?

Summary

External and internal barriers are holding Her in. You've built barriers around you for safety, security and comfort. Some you built for yourself. Many you built in order to keep others safe, secure and comfortable. A close examination of your barriers will allow you to chip away at them. Looking at them in a new light may even lead you to detonate them completely.

Reflection Questions:
Recognizing and Removing Barriers to Her

- Revisit your Story from the Intermission. Can you pinpoint where barriers were erected throughout your life?

- Write out the list of your barriers, both internal and external.

- What are the top three external barriers that are in your way? What resources do you need (time, money, help from others) to help break down those barriers?

- What are the top three internal barriers that are in your way? What triggers them and how are you coping? How willing are you to question, examine and tear down these internal barriers?

- Who gets to see you? What barriers are you putting up to keep others in the dark from the real you?

- What support or help might be necessary for you to work through the barriers?

Barrier-Busting Ideas

- **Write it down.** The next time this barrier pops up, write down what the internal dialogue is telling you. Simply writing things down often takes away the power they hold over you.

- **Talk it out.** Find a Let Her Out companion who will support you as you examine and remove these barriers. It's amazing what saying things out loud to a loving person can do to bolster your progress.

- **Build your mental muscles**. The Positive Intelligence work of master coach Shirzad Chamine has brought me into the mental gym almost as much as the physical gym on this barrier-busting journey. The way to build mental muscles is to take short, micro breaks throughout the day to focus on specific physical sensations. Every time you wash your hands, focus intently on the temperature of the water or the feeling of the lather on your hands. In between work tasks or meetings, set a timer for two minutes to do deep breathing. When you are feeling stress come over your body, gently rub two finger tips together for a minute. When you are meeting with someone and feel yourself becoming distracted, pick a visual focal point that will keep you fully present, like their eyes or their hair. Continual practice builds your executive functioning muscles and over time, you have less of a desire to fight or flee, and instead can be in the moment from a place of calmness and clarity.

- **Go deeper with a professional**. Seek out the assistance of a certified coach or mental health professional if you are ready to do deep work. A mental health professional will help you heal from the past. A coach will help you move forward.

Download the Barrier-Busting guide at LetHerOut. com/resources.

Now that you've taken a giant step forward by recognizing what could be in your way, there is only one thing left to do: Let Her Out.

Section 4

LET HER OUT

Let Her Out

By this point in the book, I hope you are eager to kick through the barriers and Let Her Out. For you, the process might be a single point-in-time decision to embrace Her and step onto a podium for the world to see. I am cheering you on as you step into the light. Or perhaps, as it was for me, Letting Her Out will be a gradual process. I was able to get closer to Her once I brought back a few of the activities and passions that lit Her up. These small steps culminated in the Leap, which is where this book will end, in the hopes that it inspires many new beginnings. Once I remembered, reconnected, and removed the barriers to Her, here is the path I took to Let Her Out.

CHAPTER 14

Letting Her Out through Writing

The first step I took to Let Her Out was starting the Small Town Leadership blog in 2016. Only one year into writing, I had published 40 blogs (25,000 words - almost equivalent to this book) and learned the following:

It's okay to put yourself out there – Early on, I hesitated and second guessed before hitting the 'Publish' button. That feeling has subsided and only surfaces when I am writing something that is highly personal. So far, no one has trolled or gotten into a debate over my content and I feel great that I am finally putting my stories into the world.

Find what sparks joy and follow it – I've written a lot about things that sparked joy for me when I was younger, most notably public speaking and music. Reminiscing made me take action to put those things back into my life through quarterly speaking gigs and joining the church choir.

My family is my foundation – My parents, sister, husband, daughters, grandparents, Uncle Bob, and neighbors were main characters in my blog. It's made me appreciate every one of them even more.

Now, more than ever, we need to understand our differences – The fastest I have written and posted a blog was November 9, 2016 following the presidential election. (It's still out there at smalltownleadership.com/election.) While I never intended to be a political blogger, I realized that having a platform gives me an opportunity to share those strongly held opinions in order to create the type of world I want my children to live in.

Letting Her Out through writing has been the equivalent of putting the "I'm not opinionated, I'm always right" button my parents gave me when I was eight, back into play. The Her who writes is strong in her beliefs and clear in her position. Life is too short to water down our words when they can bring power to others.

CHAPTER 15

Letting Her Out through Creating

While I've recounted my first manual jobs earlier in this book, I haven't described my first entrepreneurial venture as a kid. My grandparents, who retired from farming by the time I was in elementary school, took their crafting hobby on the road and began participating in craft shows and flea markets. My grandfather made miniature replica horses and wagons and my grandmother painted wooden crafts. At the same time, when I was eight or nine, I was into friendship bracelets and worry dolls.

When my collection outgrew what was acceptable for my own use, and when all of my friends had been appropriately outfitted with a friendship bracelet in their favorite colors and had a worry doll in their image, I began selling them at the craft shows my grandparents attended. Because the shows were usually during school days or farther than I would go on a weekend, I would make sure that my grandparents had a solid inventory before heading off to the next show. They would return and give me any remaining inventory and my payment. I'd like to tell you that this ended up covering my college tuition or my designs were picked up by a national brand, but no, I simply had a bit of spending money, which was usually spent at JoAnn Fabrics to replenish my supplies.

I was always creating as a kid. It helped that my parents were also creators. My dad is a county fair grand champion cross stitcher and my mom sews, cooks, and makes seasonal crafts to be admired. I continued to create as I left my small town for college and beyond – whether it was making wall art to put on my dorm room wall, pillows for my first apartment, or pictures for my baby's nursery.

Somewhere in the past 10 years, while my life has been consumed with motherhood and business building, my creativity took a backseat. Then, one day a few years ago, I realized that creating is part of who I am and that my daughters were following suit. After my oldest daughter had a meltdown when she didn't win a plush donut at an amusement park, I told her she could use her allowance to buy one. We found some online, but they were either too small, too big, too low quality, or too expensive. That's when my husband looked at me and said, "You can sew, why don't you make one?" Typically, in a previously sleep deprived state, I would have looked at him like he was crazy. This time, I said, "Sure, let's do it". A trip to JoAnn Fabrics and, a week later, my kids had their very own plush donuts.

The result of this desire to craft means that my house looks like a disaster zone. At different points in our crafting adventures, the kitchen turned into Rainbow Loom central. In the dining room there have been Perler beads, puzzles and Legos. Typically, my OCD or neat freak nature would have set in and everything would be in the appropriate bins, boxes and cabinets. But the experience of making the donuts reminded me that I want to instill a sense of creating, as opposed to consuming, in my house. This allows me to see the disarray as a canvas in mid-painting.

We spend so much time consuming – both media and goods – that we've forgotten how important it is to create. The next time you can choose between buying or creating, try the create route. You may end up with a Pinterest fail, but you'll have made a memory, and perhaps sharpened your creativity along the way. And it might be the path to take to Let Her Out.

CHAPTER 16

Letting Her Out through Relationships

One of the delights in my 30s was the arrival of people who I call "surprise friends in adulthood." There was one particular day when I was preparing a weekly entry for 52 Weeks of Meaningful Connections (which I discussed in Section 3 on the Barrier of Disconnection) and the following things happened.

8:00 a.m.: Open text from SV with a link to an article titled, "If you've wondered why you've lost friends in adulthood, this is probably why." She thought it seemed like something for Small Town Leadership.

8:10 a.m.: Open my weekly email from my good friend Katie of Team Awesome and she included this: "Have any friends you've been missing lately? Honestly, I'm not super good at keeping in touch. It also doesn't mean that I lose any love in the meantime. I have a few friends that I might only talk to a few times a year, but it's like no time has been lost. Thank you to those friends who still love me months apart when I hibernate."

8:30 a.m.: Facebook memories remind me "On this day" one year ago, I was visiting my friend, Gina, during a business trip to Birmingham, Alabama. She was someone I spent only 36 hours with the year before, but within a minute of our lunch date reunion, it was like no time had passed.

Each of these women is a *surprise friend in adulthood*. We met at work and in coach training and could have kept our relationships surface-level. However, in each of these cases, we dug into friendships, found ways to stay connected over time-zone differences, new jobs and phases in parenthood. The beauty: we can pick right back up from where we left off the last time we spoke.

For a long time, I thought I was set in the friend department. I've got nearly 1,000 on Facebook, 3,000 on LinkedIn and a few hundred more across Instagram and Twitter. Plus, when you add in a busy family and professional life, who has time for more friends? After all, it takes effort and emotional commitment to form and sustain friendships in adulthood. SV, Katie and Gina allowed me to embrace the abundance mindset when it comes to friendship. There is always space for the right person.

Now that I've overcome a limiting belief that I can't have any more friends in my life, I'm always thinking about the connections I'm forming with new people. In some cases, there is no desire to move from surface to meaningful connection. When there is a spark or a realization that we have things to learn from one another, I'm willing to get creative and make sure we find the time to connect. Sometimes it is a 20-minute catch-up call during a commute or on the sideline during my kids' soccer or softball practice. Other times it's sneaking out of the house during the kids' bedtime routine to grab a glass of wine and a couple hours of conversation.

When there is a spark or a realization that we have things to learn from one another, I'm willing to get creative and make sure we find the time to connect.

Each of these women, and even more than I have the space to write about in this book, has been a crucial part of the process to Let Her Out. We allow each other to see one another fully. We don't hold back. We go all in when it comes to a relationship, which in turn, creates these surprise friendships in adulthood.

Pause & Reflect: Let Her Out

- Do you have something to share, but are holding back? What would it take to put yourself out there?

- How could you experience more joy in your life?

- What creative pursuit puts you in flow?

- What can you do to explore how creating can bring more of Her into your life?

- Who are you spending time with that makes Her emerge? How can you invite them into your process to Let Her Out?

- Who are you spending time with that sends Her to the back of the line or into a corner? How can you evaluate your relationships to make sure you are each bringing out the best in one another?

CHAPTER 17

Let Her Out: The Leap

There I was, attending yet another event for high-potential associates at work. It was a session meant for brainstorming and innovation, which was ironic because, at that moment, I felt more stuck than I had ever been in my career. I was 35, had recently received the best review and biggest bonus of my career, and all I could feel was "meh". It's a highly technical term that most of my coaching clients have experienced at one point or another. During the lunch break, one of the facilitators, Michelle, sat next to me. Something about her made me feel safe and open and I spilled my guts that I knew there was something more for me in my career and life. She then disclosed that, in addition to facilitating events like the one we were in, she was also a coach. Could she help me out? A few days later, we got on the phone and I was able to do the gut-spilling thing to an even greater level. She explained that she helped people move through the "meh" (my words, not hers) and could likely help me get my groove back. She was hired.

Michelle and I worked together for six months. Many of the questions she asked me in coaching are similar to the ones I've posed to you in this book. What lit you up as a child? What activities had heart and meaning for you? When I told Michelle that what I missed most was speaking and writing, she challenged me to do more of it. I mapped out a plan to speak quarterly in 2016 outside of my corporate job. Within a month of setting this goal, I had four opportunities booked, with one even paying a small honorarium. This progress felt amazing. I still knew there was something bigger. I made myself think deeper about my love of speaking and writing. What was it that I spoke about that audiences loved? What were the things I longed to write about? Everything came back to Republic, Ohio. This was when I realized that I had my thought pattern all wrong up until this point in adulthood. I was telling myself that being from a small town was what was holding me back. All along, being from a small town was what propelled me forward. That's when the lightbulb came on for me. My style of leadership was small town. I like getting to know people, their stories, their pain, and their triumph. I am eager to pitch in and roll up my sleeves for a good cause. I am either all in or all out. These are the small town leadership lessons that allowed me to succeed from the biggest college campus in the country to Silicon Valley and into the Fortune 100. That's how Small Town Leadership was born. That was the beginning of Letting Her Out.

I had my thought pattern all wrong up until this point in adulthood. I was telling myself that being from a small town was what was holding me back. All along, being from a small town was what propelled me forward.

I wasn't going to bore you with the details of what it took to launch Small Town Leadership, but I realize for many of you who might be like me, you have ABSOLUTELY NO IDEA what it takes to start a business or a website, so I'm going to describe the steps I took to bring Small Town Leadership to life. I was listening to a podcast one day and the guest said, "I had an idea and went out to GoDaddy to see if the domain was available."

"So that's how you do it?" I said silently to myself. That night, I checked on GoDaddy to see if the domain for smalltownleadership.com was available. It was not. Someone else owned it. That's when I learned lesson #1 about running your own business. You can hire anyone to do anything. GoDaddy, given a dollar amount with which to negotiate, was able to purchase the domain on my behalf for $400. From there, I taught myself how to use WordPress. I tried and failed and tried again to build the website that was living in my brain. The day I got the site to "work" was one of the most satisfying days of my life. I built something that had heart and meaning for me, and I knew it could somehow change the world. From the moment I hit 'Publish', the sky was the limit in terms of what Small Town Leadership could be.

On March 16, 2016, I let the world (or at least my social media connections) know about Small Town Leadership. The support I received was immediate. People are eager to see other people chase after their dreams. Of course, there were those who were curious and nosy. What was my end goal? Was I going to quit my job? How was I going to make money? If only I knew the answers to those questions at that time.

A few months into this journey as a blogger, I met with a new acquaintance at work. He was apparently the guru for all things coaching. One of the first questions he posed to me was, "Have you ever considered becoming a coach?" My immediate response was, "Not really, but you are the fifth person who has asked me that. Maybe it's time for me to consider." Within a week, I had enrolled in the Institute for Professional Excellence in Coaching (iPEC) to become a Certified Professional Coach.

As I prepared to go to coaching school, I continued writing small town stories, got on small stages, and accepted small fees for my work. I was happy and content. This was the start of something. What, I couldn't tell at the time, but I knew it had the potential to be big.

I started coach training the week of the 2016 presidential election. This book is not about politics and not meant to send anyone running for the hills, but to say that I was stunned by the election of Donald Trump would be an understatement. I thought when I entered coach training the Friday following the election that I would be part of a big group therapy session about the state of our country. As it turns out, no mention of the election happened at all during that first weekend of coach training. What did happen is that I learned about the art of asking questions. I learned about the difference between fear, anger, and taking responsibility. I was asked to write down my goals.

I signed my very first coaching client the Monday after I returned home from training. I'll never forget how I went from coach-in-training to paid coach with one phone call. I received an email the week before coach training from someone who attended one of my speaking engagements the previous summer. She remembered me talking about my coach and asked if I could provide a referral. As I was about ready to make the connection, I thought to myself, "I am a coach" and I offered her my services. After meeting at a Starbucks for an initial consultation, we ended up working together for several months. I had no systems in place, so I was paid in cash and gift cards. Some restaurant owners hang the first dollar they earn above the register. In a similar fashion, I keep that first cash payment tucked away in a place where only I can find it.

Despite the momentum of speaking engagements and a paid coaching client, I kept freezing in fear. The moment when I settled into my dreams of speaking on big stages and coaching executive-level clients, life would get in the way. I would have a big assignment at work. My girls would have a school project or extracurricular activity that needed attending to. She was still being held in.

In the summer of 2017 I completed my 300+ hours of training and practice coaching and earned my Certified Professional Coach designation. Working with a peer coach was a huge perk of this process and I knew I wanted to continue working with a coach. As luck would have it, Apryl Schlueter of The Cheerful Mind was beta testing a new group coaching concept and I agreed to test out her program. She helped me set up my systems and processes (no more payments in gift cards and cash). I set up a formal e-newsletter system so I could easily follow-up with audiences who heard me speak and connect to people who were eager to follow my blog. (I still send out this e-newsletter on a bi-weekly basis and would love for you to be on the list. Go to smalltownleadership.com/blog to sign up.)

I decided that 2018 was the year I was going to spread my wings, cut the corporate cord, and go out into business on my own. Right at the time I was building these plans, and more importantly, the confidence that was required to put them into action, I had a meeting with a leader at my company. I laid out my plans. He was curious and open about what I was building, but also told me that he would be hiring a Director of Coaching in a few months. Might I consider applying? I told him, "Likely no, but please let me know when the job description is posted".

A couple of months passed. During the spring of 2018, my mom received a breast cancer diagnosis. The same day that I was scheduled to drive home to go to her first oncology appointment was the day this job posted. The job was everything I could ask for as my next professional step. The job description included things like: Speak and write about coaching to large audiences. Help company leaders develop coaching skills. Modernize curriculum for adult learners. Motivate a team of professional coaches.

The entire drive to my parents I was scared. I didn't know what "next" meant for our family, let alone my career. During the doctor's appointment, my mom received the best possible diagnosis and would likely beat the cancer without too much of a fight. The entire drive home, after expressing my gratitude about the news our family received that day, I thought about my next steps. It seemed too coincidental that this job popped up right when I was contemplating jumping ship. Something pulled me to the work, the team, and the leadership opportunity. I applied for the job and included the following paragraph in the cover letter, originally written in my five year vision statement as part of coach training:

"I work with leaders and executives on creating a culture that their employees, members and customers flock to. There are thousands, if not millions of people who want to be "free from." I started asking the question: What if companies were places where people wanted to "belong to?" And what if people were given the tools to help them understand it's up to them to get this feeling in their life and work? I bring these tools to companies as a way for them to develop their talent. One of the quotes that inspired this coaching niche was "What if we develop our employees and they leave?" Response: "What if we don't and they stay?"

I coach individuals who think they need to leave their corporate job to find fulfillment. In many cases, my clients have left to pursue other passions or have changed organizations. In other cases, my coaching has provided the insight that they can be a catalyst for change within their organizations. I am fulfilled knowing that I have been part of a journey for these clients who are not only improving their own quality of life, but in many cases, others in their companies."

For the first time in my career, I decided to Let Her Out. If I was going to postpone the spreading of my wings, what I could do was to show my true colors from day one in that role. Until that point in time, I felt like I had to hide what I was doing outside of work. I felt like I had to downplay the fact that I had big dreams, a platform built, and a growing base of clients and followers who were cheering me on.

This "being me" worked, because, after a long interview process, I was offered the role. Soon after taking this job, I joined the Recognized Expert Group led by Dorie Clark, an expert in personal branding and professional reinvention. After she learned my story, including my big day job and my Small Town Leadership side hustle, she asked if she could interview me for a feature in *TD Magazine*, the largest global publication in the training and development field. I said yes immediately, but also was immediately gripped with fear. Being featured in her piece, "Establish Your Side Hustle" meant I had to engage corporate public relations. It meant I had to blend my two worlds together. The day came when I sent the article to PR for their approval. I was sure someone would come to me and say, "We changed our mind, this can't be published" or, "On second thought, don't let them mention where you work." Neither was the case and the response I got was the equivalent of "looks good." At that moment, I had another major ah-ha realization. Until then, I thought if I shined a light on what I was doing outside of my day job, the company would take it away. When that didn't happen after that national exposure, I adopted a new thought:

I will shine a light on what I do outside of work in order to make what I do at work even more powerful.

Wouldn't you know that, from that moment forward, I started signing more private coaching clients and booking more speaking engagements, while at the same time was asked to lead exciting work and speak on big stages within my company? The Letting Her Out was underway.

The two years I spent in that job were the perfect launching point for me to move into my own business full time. I led what is, perhaps, the most sophisticated corporate coaching program in the Fortune 100, while also building Small Town Leadership. I spoke on big stages at work while I crafted my own keynotes to be delivered on vacation days and lunch breaks. I taught the art of coaching to new leaders at work, while helping established leaders become who they have always been in my private coaching practice. I recorded video content on a weekly basis and shared it widely. I was Letting Her Out.

In the spring of 2019, I hired yet another coach, Jeffrey Shaw, who helped me see how big Small Town Leadership could be. Because his path prior to coaching was as a professional portrait photographer, he was able to envision a path forward for my work and brand in ways I couldn't see. He didn't care what was going on in my 9-to-5 job or how much business I was booking in my side business. Jeff kept his eye on the horizon and pulled my vision in that direction, too. He allowed me to think big and take bold action.

There was still something holding me back from living full out, though. There was a sense of obligation to a company where I spent 12 years. There was a sense of security that comes from a stable job at a Fortune 100 company. There was an attachment to my ego that said, "you are the only one who can do this work." What I finally realized was this was all a load of bullcrap.

With this realization came a sense of excitement and anticipation. I set a "quit date" in my head and began getting everything in place to submit my formal resignation. Then COVID-19 hit. The day I intended to resign my position was the day the Governor of Ohio started shutting our state down. I retreated quickly, letting only a few people in on my master plan. Once again, I told myself I could wait. My dream could wait for a better time. It seemed reasonable that I could pause the Letting Her Out while the world spun on its side.

My dream could wait for a better time.

Except I couldn't. This time, I could not shake my dream. I could not keep Her in.

At midnight, during one of my writing sessions, I looked up from the screen and I asked myself the following question: Who quits her job in the middle of a global pandemic? My answer: **Someone whose dreams are bigger than her fears.** I was this person. I knew that, for me, Letting Her Out fully meant taking this step, making the leap and declaring myself "on my own."

For my entire life, I allowed my connection to outside entities, along with all of the barriers discussed in Section 3, to keep her in, hold her back, and make her play small. I am a devoted, loyal and dedicated person and have always found a way to make everyone and everything around me come first. Part of Letting Her Out is recognizing that we can put ourselves on that list, too.

When I declared my professional independence on June 26, 2020, I felt my wings fully expand for the first time in my adult life.

She was back.

The one who danced without fear of judgement.

The one who wore the crop tops.

The one who got messy.

The one who didn't apologize for her opinions.

The one who chose how she would spend her time and who she would let into her orbit.

While my journey to Letting Her Out has been about finding the courage to follow a different professional path than I ever intended, it's also been a journey of connection, reflection, friendship, love and joy. What I have realized on the path to making this leap and Letting Her Out is that when I shrink, others can't grow. The same is true for you.

When you shrink, others can't grow.

The world needs you to embrace all of you. No one benefits when your head is down, your voice is low, and your fire is extinguished. In a world where we have all Let Her Out and reclaimed who we have always been, we can all grow.

This is where this chapter concludes, but it begs for a sequel, companion series, or at the very least a 'to be continued'...I want the next volume to be your story, your Remembering, Reconnecting, Recognizing and Removing Barriers and Letting Her Out. In order to get there, put all of the pieces together from this book and take action on your Let Her Out Plan.

Build Your Let Her Out Action Plan

The journey I have taken to Let Her Out might be very similar to your path, or it could be a night-and-day difference. No matter the similarities or diversions, the following questions are universal on your quest to reclaim who you have always been.

- What does Letting Her Out look like and feel like to you? What small steps can you start taking today to remind yourself?
- What does a day in your life look like when she has been fully let out?
- What activities or hobbies do you want to introduce or reintroduce into your life?
- What opportunities can you create for yourself on our quest to Let Her Out?
- What work do you need to do to continue recognizing and removing barriers to Her?
- What do you need to do to declare that your dreams are greater than your fears?
- What will you feel like when she is free?
- What does the world look like to you when all of the women have decided to Let Her Out?

Now what? You made it through dozens of questions, and hopefully have pages of answers and responses. The next step is to take one step. And another step. And then another. Go back to the beginning and revisit the How to Use this Book section. Now that you've made it through the book, who can you share this journey with? What additional support do you need to complete the journey?

I am cheering for you as you work toward your BREAKTHROUGHS, your LEAPS, and most importantly, as you step into the world, having reclaimed who you have always been.

MY WISH FOR
ALL THE WOMEN
IN THE WORLD

My Wish for All the Women in the World

When I feel, I write. When I'm stuck, I write. When I want something, I write. As I close this book, I'm writing to each of you reading this book. I'm writing to my daughters - and all of the daughters. I'm writing to those small town girls sitting in their bedrooms next to their 4-H ribbons. I'm writing to the women of the world who are ready to Let Her Out. Here are my letters to you. Carry these with you as you continue on your path to Remember Her, Reconnect to Her, Remove the Barriers to Her, and ultimately, Let Her Out.

A letter to my daughters

Dear Mary Beth and Katie -

I don't ever want your gender to define you, limit you or make you afraid. I want you to be who you are.

I want you to make crafts and do flips and dance at parades. I want you to burp and get messy. I want you to be good at math and science and not give up when things get hard. I want you to love and protect your body.

I want you to dream big dreams and make even bigger plans. I want you to make mistakes. I want you to help others and I want you to ask for help when you need it.

I want you to be ambitious. I want you to stand up for your beliefs. I want you to be a voice for those who need you. I want you to hold me accountable to do these things alongside you.

Being a woman makes us part of a community like no other. Being ourselves is how we make our mark in this community and in our world.

Be strong. Be brave. Be you. Every day I will celebrate you.

Love,
MOMMY

Dear Small Town Girl

Dear small town girl,

You might be reading this sitting in your carefully decorated bedroom. Your trophies from last track season are getting a bit dusty. The 4-H ribbons you've had hung on your wall since you joined the local club when you were eight are starting to fade. Your bulletin board has pictures of your best friends, your summer camp memories, and your dream college list. Your favorite playlist is going – a mix of Top 40 and Hot Country. Pictures of faraway places and posters of inspirational quotes and your favorite movies cover most of the pastel walls.

You might be wondering: Where do I go from here? From this small bedroom? From this small town? What if I can't get out? What if I don't want to leave?

I'm here to tell you that you will surprise yourself in what those answers are going to be when you look back in twenty years. Maybe you'll go off to college and return home to make your small town the type of place you want to raise your family. Maybe you'll head off to a big city and not look back. **Right now, because you don't know what's possible, you don't know what's possible.**

It's up to you to figure out what your possible is. Be strong, write down your dreams, and act on those dreams.

- Want a full ride to college? Make a plan to make it happen.
- Want to travel the world? Find one place to start.
- Want to help those less fortunate than you? Start in your own town.

I'll write a letter to your older self soon. In the meantime, enjoy driving on open roads, the barn parties (be safe, of course), speak up when you see a way to make things better in your community, and always remember your roots. In whatever you do, keep Her out.

Take care,
A (slightly older) small town girl

A letter to those who are Letting Her Out

Dear friend,

Every morning when you wake up, I want you to look into the mirror and say: I see you, beautiful girl.

On the days that you are hiding from the world, or perhaps begging to be seen by the world, remember that being seen starts with YOU. If you can see YOU in all of your bravery, boldness, and brilliance, the world will eventually catch up to you. If you own who you are and see yourself as you have always been meant to be, there is nothing holding Her back.

It's never too late to Let Her Out. As you close the pages of this book, my hope is that you take steps every day to Remember Her, Reconnect to Her, and Remove the Barriers to Her.

I want to live in a world where YOU are YOU.

Thank you for allowing me to share my story. I can't wait to hear yours!

Wishing you a life with Her,
Natalie

The Birth and Completion of this Book

Along my path to the Leap, I was putting myself out there for opportunities on big stages, especially locally organized TEDx stages. Anytime a local TEDx program was announced, a few people reached out encouraging me to apply. That is exactly what I did. I applied in 2016 and was rejected. I applied in 2017 and made it to an in-person audition. I was rejected. I applied in 2019 and was told I got "really, really close", but as my mom would say, close only counts in horseshoes and hand grenades. In a surprise move, a TEDx women's event was announced in my market in 2019 and I had the perfect idea. It was a talk called "Let Her Out: Reclaim Who You Have Always Been." I thought an idea that combined diary entries with real coaching would speak to this audience of women and girls. I made it to the interview. And I was rejected.

In November of 2019, I was sitting in the lobby of a hotel in New York City a few days post-rejection and remembered that a women's conference where I spoke for the past two years had a call for presentations due within the hour. In all manner of speed and dexterity, I cut and pasted parts of the TEDx audition into the speaker submission form from my iPhone. Thanksgiving and Christmas came and went. In January, I received notification that the group would like me to present the content at the June conference.

The more I thought about building the presentation, the bigger it got. I was excited about this idea and had it accepted as a keynote for three additional conferences in 2020. Then COVID-19 hit. All of the events were cancelled. I had a choice to make. I could either fold in on this idea (perhaps those rejections were a sign) or I could build my own stage. I decided I would build my own stage and set-up my own virtual keynotes to be delivered from my home office to whoever wanted to show up on a Wednesday night in April. As I prepared for and delivered that keynote, I felt on fire. To prepare, I read each of my diaries from cover-to-cover. I realized I was sitting on a gold mine. That's when I decided Let Her Out was more than a 15-minute virtual presentation or hour-long keynote. It was certainly more than a rejecTED 10-minute talk. This was going to be my first book. This was going to be a movement.

The day after I delivered my virtual keyonte, on the made-up stage I created, I hired book coach, Cathy Fyock. She is known for helping people take their blog to book. If she could help people with this, I was certain she could help me translate my diaries to a book. Within our first session, she helped me develop my outline and I was off to the races. My first draft was done by May 2020. I delivered the copy to the editorial board in July.

Fast forward to today, August 29, 2020. I am at home in Republic, Ohio. The manuscript is due to my publisher on August 31, 2020. I bring the final copy of the book. I settle into the living room where I wrote so many of my early essays and 4-H demonstrations to put the finishing touches on this book. I close my laptop at 11pm. It is finished.

Life has a way of coming full circle. All of my rejections led to the book you are holding in your hand. All of the diary entries you read in this book were penned in the pink-heart wallpapered bedroom next to where I sit and type these final words. This small house in this small town is where SHE was made.

There is always a silver lining if we look close enough. Here's to a life full of turning rejection into new opportunities. I can't wait to see what stages you build for yourself as you Let Her Out!

Summary of Questions
from the Book

Pause, Reflect & Take Action: Photos of Her
- Action Item: Where can you find pictures of Her? If you don't have access to photos, what images can help you remember Her?
- Once you locate pictures, find one that truly represents Her as you wish to remember Her. What about Her in this picture do you appreciate?
- What about Her do you see in yourself today?

Pause, Reflect & Take Action: Diaries & Archives
- What diaries, essays, early writings or yearbooks do you have access to in order to remember Her?
- What "All About Me" works can remind you of what she liked, who her friends were, and what she did in her spare time?
- If you didn't keep a journal or don't have access to archives like these, what books or movies from the formative years in your life help you remember Her?

Pause, Reflect & Take Action: Remembering the Song in Your Heart
- What was the equivalent of piano lessons, marching band or high school musical for you? What activities brought out the song in your heart?
- What type of music, band, or song allows you to remember Her? Go turn it on!

Reflection Questions: Remember Her
- What artifacts or archives can you dig through to Remember Her?

Your own diaries or journals? Scrapbooks? Yearbooks? Photo albums? Newspaper clippings? Home videos?

- In the absence of your own archives or diaries, what was happening in the world during your formative years to help you Remember Her? What movies, music and world events can help you remember?
- What do you remember about the Her you see in photos from your childhood? How often is she making an appearance in adulthood?
- What parts of your childhood do you reminisce about the most? What memories will your children never experience because life isn't as it used to be?
- What were your "streaks of happiness" moments that can help you remember Her? How are you actively looking for and appreciating streaks of happiness in our current day-to-day lives?
- How did your ambition show up as a child? Were you on the leader-board for Girl Scout cookie sales? Did you coordinate ad-hoc community service projects when your neighbors were in need? Where does that ambition show up today? Where is it suppressed today?
- What moments from your younger days can you relive in order to remember Her?
- Who can you talk to or visit with who will help you remember Her? Siblings, family members, friends, teachers?
- What problems were you solving at a young age for pure joy and fun? How are you still solving similar problems today?
- What did you want to be when you grew up that didn't make sense to you at the time? How does it fit into your passion or profession today?

Pause & Reflect: Reconnecting to Your Voice
- How do you define the voice of your youth? Even if you didn't take the microphone or win any purple ribbons, you had moments when your voice was strong, your ideas were clear, and you felt like you were on top of the world. What were those moments?
- What can you find to remind you of your voice from your youth? Do you have a box of middle and high school essays that can connect you to the sage (or silly) things you said in your youth? Do you have a digitized copy of your early public speaking performances?

Pause & Reflect: Reconnecting to Your Strength
- How do you remember Her physical strength? What about Her mental strength?
- What teams were you on that help you reconnect to Her?
- What teams were you cut from or didn't dare try out for and how did that shape Her?
- What is a moment when you took control of your strength and your body?

Pause & Reflect: Reconnecting to Young Love
- How do you remember young love?
- What prom photos or love notes do you need to pull out of storage to connect to long-ago-love?
- Who stole your heart only to have you take it back?
- Who still holds a piece of your heart in theirs?
- How did you experience other types of love, like love for friends, family, and community, in your youth? How did that shape you?

Reflection Questions: Reconnecting to Your Conviction
- What are the earliest beliefs that you remember? How were they formed? How have they evolved?
- How did you decide your positions on controversial issues? How have these positions been challenged, or even changed, over the years?
- What has been your journey walking in other people's shoes?

Reflection Questions: Reconnect to Her
- What brought you joy as a child, teenager and young adult? What activity, relationship or cause made you light up a room? Write those things down in as much detail as you can. Who were you with? What was the scene?
- What 5 adjectives would you use to describe Her?
- What personality traits and characteristics do only your closest childhood friends and family members know about?
- What stories formed your early years? What were the stories of triumph?

Of tragedy? Of silliness and glee? Of normal, everyday occurrences that remind you of a simpler time?

- What have you purposely tried to forget? What opportunity do you have to reconnect instead of forget?

Reflection Questions: Recognizing and Removing External Barriers

- What external barriers are holding you back from Her?
- What action can you take to remove or minimize these barriers to bring something you used to love doing back into your life?

Reflection Questions: Moving from Finite to Infinite

- How are you caught in the rat race of a finite game?
- How is that holding Her back instead of letting Her out?
- What mindset shifts can you make to push through this barrier?

Pause & Reflect: Recognition

- How important is recognition to you?
- What is this barrier costing you in your personal and professional life?

Pause & Reflect: Emptiness

- How prevalent is the feeling of emptiness in your life?
- What is the effect on you and your relationships?
- What is one step you can take to begin breaking down this barrier?

Pause & Reflect: Dimming Ambition

- Where have you dimmed your ambition?
- What did you want to be when you grew up? Does part of you still wonder what it would be like to do that thing?
- How can you redefine ambition in order to bring Her forward?

Pause & Reflect: Impostor Syndrome

- How often are you living in fear versus stepping into opportunity?
- How often do you find yourself doubting your recognition or achievements? How can you connect to Her in order to remind yourself that you are worthy and earned the award or the recognition?

- What would your life look like if you removed the barrier of impostor syndrome and instead you stepped into the shoes of confidence? What if you enjoyed your success and accomplishments?

Pause & Reflect: Loneliness & Disconnection
- How much do you resonate with the sentiment of being "So Damn Lonely?"
- What is on your loneliness list that has built up walls to other people and meaningful relationships?
- Who can help you feel less lonely and disconnected?

Pause & Reflect: Your Body
- How have your perception and feelings about your body turned into a barrier?
- What physical challenges have you faced or overcome to remind you of your strength?
- What action do you want to take to remind yourself of your strength and power?

Pause & Reflect: Pain of Adulthood
- What is it costing you to keep everyone around you comfortable?
- What would it feel like to release some of your pain, if only to a few close friends?
- Who might benefit from hearing your story?

Pause & Reflect: Busyness of Early Parenthood
- How often are you using parenthood or your particular life stage as a barrier that prevents you from chasing your dreams?
- What is one step of the blueprint you can use to help you begin to remove the barrier?

Pause & Reflect: Power
- What does being real mean to you?
- Who gets to see you and know you?

Reflection Questions: Recognizing and Removing Barriers to Her

- Revisit your Story from the Intermission. Can you pinpoint where barriers were erected throughout your life?
- Write out the list of your barriers, both internal and external.
- What are the top three external barriers that are in your way? What resources do you need (time, money, help from others) to help break down those barriers?
- What are the top three internal barriers that are in your way? What triggers them and how are you coping? How willing are you to question, examine and tear down these internal barriers?
- Who gets to see you? What barriers are you putting up to keep others in the dark from the real you?
- What support or help might be necessary for you to work through the barriers?

Pause & Reflect: Let Her Out

- Do you have something to share, but are holding back? What would it take to put yourself out there?
- How could you experience more joy in your life?
- What creative pursuit puts you in flow?
- What can you do to explore how creating can bring more of Her into your life?
- Who are you spending time with that makes Her emerge? How can you invite them into your process to Let Her Out?
- Who are you spending time with that sends Her to the back of the line or into a corner? How can you evaluate your relationships to make sure you are each bringing out the best in one another?

Build Your Let Her Out Action Plan

- What does Letting Her Out look like and feel like to you? What are small steps you can start taking today to remind yourself of Her?
- What does a day in your life look like when she has been fully let out?
- What activities or hobbies do you want to introduce or reintroduce into your life?

- What opportunities can you create for yourself on your quest to Let Her Out?
- What work do you need to do to continue recognizing and removing barriers to Her?
- What do you need to do to declare that your dreams are greater than your fears?
- What will you feel like when she is free?
- What does the world look like to you when all of the women have decided to Let Her Out?

Acknowledgements

Writing a book is something I've said I'd do for a long time. Saying you are going to do it and actually doing it are completely different things. This book would not have been possible without the help, encouragement, and guidance of the following people:

John and Tracy - We sat together in a Starbucks in Dallas, Texas when you both declared that I'm not building a company, I'm building a movement. I haven't stopped moving forward since that day and I feel the gentle push of your hand behind me on days when I need it and I hear your voices in my head when I decide to play small. More than anything, I know you are only one phone call away from some tough love and breakthrough coaching.

Katie R - Watching you turn your TEDx talk INTO your first book was inspiring. I thought I would simply do what you did. Instead, I had to pave my own path and you have been there the entire way, steering me when needed and providing levity on tough days. I appreciate your lifelong friendship and know we are only one meme away from making each other's day better.

Shawnda V - You were the first person I printed out a section of this book and sent it to because I truly wanted to show you how much of a difference you have made in my life. I am grateful that our professional paths brought us together and even more grateful that friendship keeps us together beyond those paths.

Shawn H - You have shown me that there is no randomness in life. We were supposed to be seated next to one another at that offsite in the summer of 2017. We were meant to connect the next year. I cannot thank you enough for being the representative Him who read this book, provided thoughtful feedback that made it so much more than it would have been if you hadn't read it. Thank you for your constant care and compassion for others. You are part of the reason I was able to Let Her Out.

Abbey G, Jessica W and Olivea O - Thank you for not only agreeing to beta test Let Her Out Group Coaching, but for also agreeing to review this manuscript. Your willingness to be all in on "Let Her Out" reassures me that when we show up for each other, we all are better for it.

MB, AC, JY, LA - Thank you for being some of the first to Let Her Out. I know each of you are going to bring your whole hearted experiences into the world and make it better for everyone you encounter along the way.

Lori P - Thank you for diving diligently into these pages. I appreciate you taking yourself on the journey to Let Her Out so that the experience can be better for everyone reading it.

Michelle, Apryl and Jeff - Thank you for being the coaches I needed to help bring my full self to everything I do. Once you are my coach, you are always my coach. You are all amazing at your craft and I am grateful to have you on my Let Her Out team.

Bruce B - It's never too late to tell someone how much of a difference they've made in your life and I will tell you that every time we talk. Keep shining your light and spreading your message, whether on screen, in person, or over the airwaves.

To the Let Her Out Early Readers & Launch Crew - Thank you for the notes of encouragement, sending me your pictures of Her, and asking for more. You have no idea how your thumbs up, comments and emails helped on days when I wondered if anyone would read this book.

To Cathy Fyock - Thank you for jumping right into this process and helping point my sails in the right direction. From our first session, you were able to see the potential for this book. I appreciate you allowing me to show up in our 1:1 and group sessions with ALL of the ideas. I'm aiming higher because of your encouragement and guidance.

To Bill & Shirzad - Thank you for bringing mental fitness to the world and for bringing me into the fold. Without your work and desire to change the world, I might not have Let Her Out when I did.

To my Seneca East classmates and fellow Republic residents and alumni - We might be small town kids, but we are making big things happen in the world. You played a huge role in making me who I am today. Go Tigers!

To the women of Dublin, Ohio - Let's commit to Letting Her Out. No longer do we need to be referred to only as "so-and-so's mom", but instead as who we are and who we want to be in our community and our world. When I see you at sports practice, school events, and at the grocery store, let's get deep and be real, no matter how foreign and awkward it might feel.

To my Nationwide family - Thank you for letting me be me. That is what everyone is searching for at work. For those of you who shared a lunch or coffee break, engaged in a long term mentoring relationship, or served on the same team as me, I appreciate you allowing me to Let Her Out on the clock. I believe we are all better for that and we should encourage everyone to bring their full self to work.

To Dorie Clark and the Recognized Expert Community - I have been watching each of you own your space and claim your expertise. That's allowed me to see what is possible for me.

To Mom - Writing this book when I did helped me connect to our family in a new and different way. It was the therapy I needed at a time when remembering our family adventures and laughter seemed more important than ever. You truly are the glue that holds us all together and I don't want you ever to forget that. I might not say it out loud a lot, but hopefully holding this book in your hands is a reminder of what you have done in the world.

To Dad - While you will likely never be able to read this book or truly understand your significance as a leading character, your influence is everywhere. You taught me to talk to strangers and take the microphone. I would not be where I am today without that guidance. I will always remember you as my #1 fan.

To Nicci - Thanks for being in these stories. We will always be small town girls, but we sure are making a big difference in the world!

To Rob - You saw Her at 18 years old and knew what was possible. It's taken me 22 years to catch onto that, but now there is no turning back from Her. Together, we are unstoppable. Together, we are building a future where all of the Hers in our lives will never question their capability and potential. It starts by sharing our story.

To Mary Beth and Katie - You were usually sound asleep when I was writing this book. I know soon you will understand what this book means. I hope your takeaway is that you will never need to Let Her Out because you are going to strive to Keep Her Out from this moment forward. Someday you will appreciate my motivational quotes, dinner table and driver seat coaching, and encouragement to write your own story. You are both amazing and are my reminder that Let Her Out is more than a book, it is a movement.

To you, the reader - Thank you for taking this journey with me. I hope I have motivated and inspired you to Let Her Out. It's in your hands from here.

Stay Connected to Let Her Out

Join the movement

Let Her Out is not meant to be just a book. It's meant to be the start of a movement. Make sure you join my email newsletter list to keep up with the latest and find out about related community and coaching offerings. Visit LetHerOut.com and sign-up today.

Book Bonuses & Resources

A full array of worksheets, motivational quotes, and social media shares are available at LetHerOut.com/resources.

Share this journey

One of my favorite teachers once told me that the best way to solidify our learning is to teach what we've learned to others. What has been your greatest takeaway from this book that you will share with your family, friends and colleagues? Don't be shy about sharing (and while you are at it, tag me and #letheroutbook on all of the socials.)

Write a review

Would you consider giving it a rating wherever you bought the book? Online book stores are more likely to promote a book when they feel good about its content, and reader reviews are a great barometer of a book's quality. This would mean a lot to me as a first-time author!

Please go to the website of wherever you bought the book, search for my name and the book title, and leave a review. If able, perhaps consider adding a picture of you holding the book. That increases the likelihood your review will be accepted!

Share the Love

Get this book for a friend, associate or family member!

If you have found this book valuable and know others who would find it useful, consider buying them a copy as a gift. Special bulk discounts are available if you would like your whole team or organization to benefit from reading this. Send an email to info@letherout.com for more information.

Share Your Let Her Out Story

I believe we each have a story worth sharing. If reading this book has inspired you to reflect and write your own Let Her Out story, I'd love it if you would share it with me. Send your reflections and story to info@letherout.com.

Connect With Natalie for Speaking, Coaching & Media Appearances

If you want to bring this work even more deeply into your company, organization or personal life, consider hiring Natalie as a coach, speaker, or guest for your media platform. Find information on her services at smalltownleadership.com and send your inquiry to info@letherout.com.

Here are what previous speaking and coaching clients have to say about working with Natalie:

"That speaker was awesome! Our staff needed to hear that. How can we get more?"

"Natalie was an exceptional speaker and someone I would be excited to have as my own mentor. Her content was useful and well thought-out, and she was personable and able to connect with the attendees."

"Natalie is a wonderful facilitator and coach of the content, sharing invaluable insights for us to take with us."

"Natalie helped me fall back in love with my business."

"I would highly recommend Natalie for any coaching, team building or overall continuous improvement training. Natalie was instrumental in both my professional and personal development. Her unique coaching was tailored directly to my needs and her candid dialogue and active listening

were incomparable. Natalie has a natural coaching talent that elevated my communication practices, which allowed me to work more effectively with my team."

"Natalie's attention to detail, energy and leadership were qualities that made the coaching impactful and fun! These training sessions helped greatly during graduate school and led to promotion! I can't thank 'Coach' Siston enough for the work she has done to help get me to the next level early in my career!"

"In the middle of the pandemic, I started a coaching relationship with Natalie. At my executive level, you do coaching and get coached all the time...but this time it was important to do this professional coaching outside of work so I could bring all of me and really work through things without fear of judgment or saying the wrong thing. I brought all my fears and laid it on the table, I found things that I personally needed to work through that had been buried for years and now was impacting the next level me. Throughout this journey I felt heard, I found space to explore my feelings, my natural tendencies and spent a lot of time reflecting to re-invest in me. I am so glad I made the investment. Do the work to be a better you, you are worth it."

About the Cover & Photos in this Book

Writing this book has been fun, and bringing it to life has been just as fun. The day Cathy, my book coach, sent me her favorite childhood picture without prompting, I knew we had to see Her as part of this book. Through brainstorming sessions, creative Google form set ups, and exploration of mosaic technology with my publisher, we found a way to show many versions of Her on the cover and in these pages.

The cover mosaic and interior collages are made up of pictures of Her (and Him) sent to me by friends, family, readers and fans. These pictures show the true essence of each of these people. It's the picture they bring to mind when they want to channel Her (or Him). My extreme gratitude for giving me permission to include you in this book in this way.

Cover art concept: Will Bowman
Cover art design: Chris Simmons
Original Cover Photo: Aaron Lewis

About the Author

Natalie's career has taken her from Silicon Valley to the Fortune 100 and into entrepreneurship, but being raised in Republic, OH (population 600) is where she learned her greatest leadership lessons. Natalie uses these lessons from small town living to help leaders and organizations create big success in the world.

In addition to being a 10-year 4-H member and repeat State Fair champion in public speaking, Natalie is a two-time graduate of The Ohio State University and Professional Coach accredited through the International Coach Federation. She has 20+ years of experience coaching, developing leaders, and strengthening teams in the non-profit, higher education, and corporate sectors. She works both 1:1 and in small groups, coaching clients to help them be more connected – to themselves, their work, families, and communities. She is a frequent speaker at leadership, university, and corporate events.

Natalie resides in Dublin, Ohio with her husband, Rob, and two young daughters. When she's not writing, speaking or coaching, she enjoys mentoring students, training for endurance athletic events, and improving her golf game.

Let Her Out: Reclaim Who You Have Always Been is Natalie's first book.

Learn more at: smalltownleadership.com or letherout.com